Richar

Welsh Corgis: Pembroke and Cardigan

Everything about Purchase, Care, Nutrition, Grooming, Behavior, and Training

Filled with Full-color Photographs
Illustrations by Pam Tanzey

BARRON'S

CONTENTS

HISTORY AND ORIGIN OF WELSH CORGIS

Ancient History

In the earliest light of civilization, over 10,000 years ago, humans began to establish a relationship with a creature of the forest. That relationship was to endure and grow to become one that humans have shared with no other living thing beyond their own species.

That first meeting was between Mesolithic people and the wolf. As early people matured into the intelligent and civilized beings they are today, so did the wolf accompany them through their transitions to become not only servant but also what many humans were to call their best friend. *Canis lupus*, the wolf, became *Canis familiaris*, the dog.

Controversy exists as to whether today's domestic dog descended solely from the wolf family or if an admixture of jackal and other wild canine blood assisted in this transition. It is generally conceded, however, that four main canine groups evolved from different branches of the wolf family.

These four groups have been given different names by different historians, but Richard and Alice Fiennes' *The Natural History of Dogs* categorizes descendants of the ancient dog as follows:

The Mastiff Group descended primarily from mountain wolves of the Tibetan wolf type and includes many of the dogs in today's sporting group classification, such as the spaniels and setters. The true scent-hunting hounds and mastiff-type dogs also descend from this group. There is evidence that some of the breeds in this group carry the blood of the spitz or northern group of wolves as well.

Typical of the Mastiff Group is a tendency to produce large floppy ears, a heavy muzzle, and an obvious stop. A dog's stop is the depression or step down in the topline of the head, situated almost centrally between the eyes where the skull meets the upper jaw. These characteristics and several others will have increased significance as we trace the development of the Cardigan Welsh Corgi down from its Deutsche Brachen (German scenthound) ancestry.

The Dingo Group descended from the Asian wolf and includes the Basenji, the Rhodesian Ridgeback (albeit with many crosses to European breeds), and many of the pariah breeds existing in the Near, Middle, and Far East, as well as in Africa. Even at their least domesticated stage this group appears to have been far more tractable and easily able to coexist with humans.

The Greyhound Group claims an extremely fleet of foot Asian wolf relative as its source. Here we find all the sighthounds—the Afghan

Add a bit of hair, a fox-brush tail, and upright ears to the Dachshund, and its relationship to the Cardigan Corgi does not stretch the imagination.

Hound, the Borzoi, the Irish Wolfhound, and the Greyhound—among them.

The Northern Group claims the northern wolf as its predecessor. Included here are most of the breeds associated with the extreme conditions of the cold climates. Among them we find the arctic type, the terriers, and the spitz

The need for a herding dog short-statured enough to avoid the flying hooves of cattle led to the development of the early Corgi breeds in Wales.

breeds. The Pembroke Corgis are included in this group through their spitz ancestors.

Early humans had little need to train the *wolf-cum-dog* descendants of this group to herd the livestock they kept. Wolves had been rounding up and separating their prey for countless centuries. The task of humans was to produce a herder that would not bring down and devour what it herded! It appears that descendants of the more docile Dingo Group had influence in this respect.

The frigid conditions of the Scandinavian countries dictated that the earliest inhabitants economize in all things including the dogs they kept. These people, who later included the Vikings themselves, developed many breeds of dogs suitable to those conditions. The Scandinavian breeds were hardy working breeds, some markedly hound types of varying sizes, others of spitz descendency.

There is documented evidence the Vikings took along their dogs on their journeys across the North Sea to Wales. One need only look at some of the breeds native to the Scandinavian countries to see how they might have influenced the development of the two Corgis in the British Isles.

Horses for Courses

"Horses for courses" is an old saying among British stockmen that has served as the basis for development of many kinds of prized livestock.

Translated into layman's terms, this adage simply means choosing a formula that will produce a horse best suited to the terrain of the region in which the horse will work. This formula not only applied to horse breeding but was the basis upon which many of Great Britain's outstanding dog breeds were developed.

Pembrokeshire and Cardiganshire were agricultural areas in Wales. For the most part the farms were situated among the rather infertile and rocky hills. The weather was often wild, wet, and windy, and a breed of tough black cattle was developed to cope with these inhospitable conditions.

It is believed that both the modern Dachshund and today's Cardigan Welsh Corgi had their roots in Germany's Deutsche Brachen dogs.

Fences to confine the surly beasts were not practical or affordable. Still, the cattle had to be located and brought in at milking time. The dog could not be large and costly to maintain nor was a large dog practical around the ill-tempered cattle whose flying hooves could easily land a well-directed rear kick to the head of a large dog.

What was needed was a small dog, short enough to duck under a flying hoof and nip at the cow's other hoof that was planted on the ground. The head had to have a flat skull for exactly the same reason. It had to be a tough little dog because the weather demanded it. A short protective weather-resistant coat was a must for the muddy conditions that continually existed.

The inhabitants of Pembrokeshire and Cardiganshire in Wales went about their separate

ways through the years to develop the kind of dog that was best suited to performing the required task under the conditions that existed in their respective areas. The Welsh called these dogs Corgis. The name Corgi generally meant "cur dog" or "dwarf dog" in Welsh. Neither name was used in the derogatory sense but rather to describe a small working kind of dog.

It is believed Cardiganshire folk used native British stock that could have been influenced by either Scandinavian or central European

The modern Cardigan Welsh Corgi.

hounds. The people in Pembrokeshire worked with dogs whose ancestors were thought to be primarily Scandinavian spitz breeds.

Few doubt the relationship of the Pembroke Corgi to its Swedish lookalike, the Vallhund.

Cardiganshire's Corgi

In Cardiganshire the Corgi was also known as *Ci Llathaid,* which meant "by the yard" relating to the Welsh measurement of a yard, which is 40 inches (101.5 cm) long. The dogs were larger than those of their neighbors in nearby Pembrokeshire. They were considerably longer in body, their front legs were bowed, and they had long bushy tails. They also stood on large round feet. They were often blue merle or brindle in color and in most cases had large drooping ears.

At least one theory of the Cardigan Corgi's history cites the scenthound breeds as having had great influence. Scenthounds are thought to have been brought from central European countries to Wales as early as 1200 B.C. If these hounds arrived at that early date they were undoubtedly of the German Deutsche Brachen type. If they arrived at a later date the ancestors could well have been the German Dachshund or Teckel that had been developed from the Deutsche Brachen dogs.

The hounds were said to have crossed with the existing "heeling" breeds of Wales. The resulting descendants were said to have had long bodies, bowed legs, and large feet that turned out, as well as the typical scenthound's pendant ear.

Somewhere in the late 1800s the Cardiganshire farmers began to replace their cattle with much more economically maintained sheep herds. The cattle-heeling instincts of their Corgis proved too harsh for the easily frightened sheep, so crosses with the less aggressive old Welsh Collie were resorted to. It is believed that this is where the blue merle color was introduced into the Cardigan gene pool.

There are many theories for the metamorphosis of the early houndlike Cardigan Corgi into a breed very similar in some respects to its cousin the Pembroke Corgi. Some believe it was done entirely without Pembroke crosses but through frequent breedings back to the many indigenous Welsh herding breeds that were prick-eared and more spitzlike in appearance. Others believe the Pembroke dog had influence on the changes that came about for the dog from Cardiganshire. Only time and further archeological discoveries will ever solve the mystery.

The Pembrokeshire Corgi

There seems to be little doubt that the Vastgotaspets (Swedish Vallhund), developed from native spitz breeds in Sweden, had an important role in the development of the Pembroke Welsh Corgi. Whether it was the breeds native to Wales that may have influenced development of the Vallhund or the Swedish breeds serving as the cornerstone for the Corgi will undoubtedly remain, at least for the present, another Corgi mystery; however, few doubt the relationship of the Corgi and the Vallhund.

The Pembrokeshire Corgi was alternately called *Ci Sodli,* which meant "to heel" or work livestock from behind by nipping at the heels. The dog was smaller than its cousin from Cardiganshire, much more compact, and its front legs fairly straight by comparison. Usually the

Except for its long legs, the Swedish Grousehunt Spitz bears a striking resemblance to the Pembroke Corgi.

Pembrokeshire dog was born without a tail. If one was born with a tail, it was docked. The head did not much differ from the Cardiganshire dog but often the coat of *Ci Sodli* was shorter and smoother and the ears were smaller.

Pembrokeshire Corgis were marvelous cattle dogs and the poor farmers depended heavily upon them to assist in eking out some kind of meager living. Like their cousins, the Pembrokeshire dogs became members of the family, working hard in the fields all day, protecting their families from danger at night by sounding the alarm, and often serving as "nannies" for the children while the parents worked in the fields. "They did everything but wait on tables," Charles Lister-Kaye and Dickie Albin jokingly stated in their study of the breed, *The Welsh Corgi*.

These farming families could never have imagined their beloved "cur dogs" would one day romp with kings and queens and be petted and pampered as show dogs in the four corners of the world. The lowly Corgi was destined for a most glamorous future.

Show Dogs

Until the early 1920s both Corgis led a hard-working but contented life on the farm, but about 1925 their destiny took an abrupt turn. Several Corgi owners gathered at a local pub and decided their dedicated companions should be included in dog shows.

Captain J. H. Howell called a meeting of breed fanciers and the Welsh Corgi Club was organized. Pedigrees were written down from memory and breed standards were agreed upon. The two Corgis, which up to that point had not yet been bred for looks, began to appear at the local shows. The dogs ran the gamut of sizes and shapes but the club was founded with a healthy 59-member charter group. These founding fanciers were interested only in the little dog from Pembrokeshire and it was that breed and that look that was promoted.

For the next decade both types—Pembrokeshire and Cardiganshire (later shortened to Pembroke and Cardigan)—were considered two varieties of the same breed and interbreeding continued. Both were shown in the same classes at dog shows.

Cardigan vs. Pembroke

Early exhibitors recall terrible rows between the Cardigan and the Pembroke fanciers. Shows were judged by specialists and when Pembroke breeders judged only Pembrokes won. Cardigan fanciers were no less loyal to their breed when they were called upon to judge.

Spitz breeds, Norwegian Elkhounds, and Pembroke Welsh Corgis (from left) claim the northern wolf as their common ancestor.

Each group felt theirs was the true Corgi type and the question was never settled nor was peace restored until 1934 when the Kennel Club in Great Britain granted separate breed status. At the time of separation, 59 Cardigans and 240 Pembrokes were registered. Dividing the breed led to the difficult task of deciding which of the two breeds each dog belonged to. Often it was decided simply by the owner choosing which breed he or she wanted to be associated with.

While all this was occurring, Mrs. Thelma Gray, a highly successful and influential dog fancier, took up the Pembroke cause under her Rozavel kennel prefix and the future of the breed was insured. Mrs. Gray had indeed inherited the stockmanship that some of the British have been blessed with when it comes to perfecting and perpetuating outstanding purebred animals.

The devotion of the Corgi fanciers to their respective breeds was severely tested when it was called upon to help the breeds survive the devastating effects of World War I. Again the indomitable spirit of the breeds' fanciers was brought to bear with the even more disastrous World War II.

The Corgi needs to be busy, whether herding sheep or people.

Championship status was first granted Welsh Corgis in 1928 at the Cardiff show, but the two were still shown as one breed. The first champion in the breed, either Pembroke or Cardigan, was the red and white Pembroke female Shan Fach, who annexed the title in 1929.

The Cardigan Corgi, especially vulnerable to the deprivation of the war years, did not fare as well as the Pembroke. Registrations dropped to only 11 for 1940 and even at the end of the war in 1945 registrations stood at 61, only two more than at the time of initial acceptance in 1934. Still, owing to the indomitable spirit of the British fancy, both breeds did manage to survive. Without missing a beat, the Welsh Corgi League, which had been founded by Thelma Gray in 1938, organized a gala championship show. The show was held at Buckingham Gate in London where the Pembrokes were joined by the Cardigan Welsh Corgi Association.

Dog of the Royal Family

There can be no doubt whatsoever that the affection of England's royal family for the Pembroke Corgi advanced the cause of the breed both in the homeland and around the world. King George VI was the first to acquire a Corgi and his Rozavel Golden Eagle ("Dookie") led the way for countless generations of Corgis to grace the halls of Buckingham Palace and Windsor, Sandringham, and Balmoral castles, all residences of the royal family.

THE CORGIS COME TO AMERICA

A Fortunate Meeting

In 1933 Mrs. Lewis Roesler (later Mrs. Edward Renner), who lived in the Berkshire Hills of Massachusetts, saw her first Pembroke Corgi at Paddington Station in London. She fell in love with the little dog, purchased her on the spot, and brought her back to the United States. Little Madam was the name of the Corgi and she is believed to be the first Pembroke Corgi officially to take residence in the United States.

Before returning to America, however, Mrs. Roesler stopped at several Corgi kennels and was able to select another Pembroke named Captain William Lewis to accompany her and Little Madam home to their Merriedip Kennels, which held a great reputation for outstanding Old English Sheepdogs. Little Madam was to become the first Corgi to be registered with the AKC when the breed (still including both Corgis as two varieties of one breed) was given official recognition in 1934.

In that same year the first Pembroke litter was registered with the AKC. The litter was owned by Mr. E. M. Tidd of Oakland, California, and was out of his female, "Toots," that he had imported from Canada. Mr. Tidd also imported the English Champion Bowhit Pivot in 1935. Pivot was the first Pembroke Welsh Corgi ever to have won a Best in Show at a British Open Show.

The excellent quality dog was registered with the AKC as Sierra Bowhit Pivot and continued his winning ways with a successful career in America. His wins included the distinction of becoming the first American champion and the first of his breed to win a Group placing in this country. Pivot was followed to the title a month later by Little Madam.

An Added Boost

In 1937 another fortunate event occurred that was to insure the breed's future in America as had happened in Great Britain. Derek Rayne, a young English expatriate residing in California, purchased Pivot from Mr. Tidd. Rayne was scion of a highly successful family of dog fanciers in his homeland, understood dogs and dog breeding extremely well, and was highly respected by the American dog fancy. Rayne piloted Pivot to many outstanding wins in California including a Group First. Pivot was seven-and-one-half years old at the time of his Group win and went on to live another ten years in great health.

By 1936 enthusiasm for the breed was increasing rapidly. The Pembroke Welsh Corgi Club of America was formed and held its first Specialty Show in the same year in conjunction with Mrs. Geraldine Dodge's famed Morris and Essex show. There is no question that holding the Corgi Specialty with Morris and Essex added to the prestige of the breed, for the event was held at the Giralda Farms estate of Mrs. Geraldine Rockefeller Dodge in Madison, New Jersey.

Unfortunately, American Corgi fanciers were also forced to endure the conditions of World War II when show and breeding activities were all but suspended. With the end of the war, the dedicated few who still remained came back with gusto.

Rise to Prominence

New imports arrived in the United States and breeding resumed. Rozavel Uncle Sam, bred in Great Britain by Thelma Gray, came to America and literally dominated the show scene. In 1949 Uncle Sam became the first Pembroke Welsh Corgi to win an all-breed Best in Show in the United States.

The Pembroke's future as a show dog in America was assured. When the Corgi was first eligible to be registered with the AKC, nine were registered. There were 135 registered in 1938, and by 1978 there were 2,349 registered in that year alone. The registration figures for 1997 reveal that 8,281 Pembrokes were individually registered with the AKC and they stood in 37th place among the 146 breeds listed that year.

Slow Cardigan Progress

A pair of Cardigans, Cassie and Cando, had arrived in Boston in 1931, but unfortunately the Cardigan Corgi fanciers were not as unified in their beliefs as the Pembroke fanciers tended to be. Constant squabbling over different opin-

ions on correct type had kept the breed immobilized in England and little progress was made. The war years did nothing to help the Cardigan cause. By the end of World War II numbers and interest had diminished to a point that the breed was almost nonexistent either in England or the United States.

The English import Blodwen of Robinscroft was the first Cardigan Welsh Corgi to be registered with the AKC. The year was 1935. Registrations have slowly and steadily increased through the years, but the breed has never achieved the show ring success of the Pembroke. In 1997 there were 752 Cardigans registered with the AKC and the breed stood in 88th place among the breeds recognized by that organization.

The Two Standards

The Pembroke Welsh Corgi Club of America and the Cardigan Welsh Corgi Club of America provide standards of excellence for their respective breeds. These standards contain, in detail, the characteristics that collectively typify the ideal specimen of each breed.

It must be remembered that no dog is perfect and no dog adheres entirely to a given breed standard. The standard is used as a guideline by which breeders and judges evaluate every dog of that breed.

A Tale of Two Corgis

Although many observers see the main difference between the two Corgis—primarily one of tails—the respective enthusiasts of each breed tell a much different tale. Most important is the fact that they are not two varieties of the same breed but two separate and distinct breeds.

Cardigan (left) and Pembroke Welsh Corgi.

Cardigan enthusiasts will quickly state that their breed has an entirely different origin than Pembroke—theirs descending from the ancient Teckel, a low-slung and dwarf-legged European dog. They also claim that the dogs from Pembrokeshire have a Nordic spitz origin. Both claim to be the true and original Corgi.

Although the Cardigan enthusiasts' position may not be easily disputed, the fact remains that the two were considered one breed and interbred in England for such an extended period that the answer to which came first and where it came from have become moot points. What is of consequence is the physical differences between the two. Tail length is not where the tale begins and ends.

Where the Differences Lie

Proportions: Cardigan. The ideal height measured from the withers (the highest point of the shoulder) to the ground is 10.5 to 12.5 inches (26.5 to 31.5 cm). The ideal length/height ratio is 1.8 to 1 measured from point of the breastbone to rear of the hip. Ideal weight for dogs is 30 to 38 pounds (13.6–17 kg); bitches 25 to 34 pounds (11–15 kg). **Pembroke.** Ideal height is 10 to 12 inches (25.5 to 30.5 cm) at the shoulder. The distance from the withers to the base of the tail should be approximately 40 percent greater than the height. Ideal weight for dogs is not exceeding 30 pounds (13.6 kg); bitches 25 pounds (11 kg).

Heads: There are only subtle differences in head and both breeds should have heads "foxy" in make and shape. **Cardigan.** The Cardigan head gives the appearance of slightly greater mass and strength with a larger, more promi-

nent nose. Nose color other than solid black, except in blue merles, is a disqualification. The Cardigan's ears are quite large for the size of the dog and drop ears are a disqualification. The eyes are required to be dark and in harmony with coat color. Only blue merles are allowed to have one or both eyes blue in color; otherwise, blue eyes are a disqualification. **Pembroke.** Pembroke ears are of medium size. The eyes are to be variations of brown in harmony with coat color. Black eyes are undesirable as are yellow or bluish eyes.

Body: Cardigan. The most obvious difference here is in the greater length and proportionately heavier bone of the Cardigan. The front construction of the Cardigan differs in that the forearm is substantially curved to fit around the ribcage. **Pembroke.** Although there is a slight bend to the Pembroke's forearm, it is not as exaggerated as in the Cardigan.

Tail: Cardigan. The Cardigan's tail must reach well below the hock and it must have a foxlike brush. **Pembroke.** The Pembroke tail is docked as short as possible without being indented.

Coat: The coats of both breeds are described similarly in the standard and anything other than a coat that serves to protect the dog from

the elements would be considered a serious fault. Extremely long soft coats are considered a very serious fault. Trimming is not permitted on either breed outside of tidying up the feet.

Color: Cardigan. The Cardigan standard allows a much wider range of colors than what is permissible with the Pembroke. Cardigans may have all shades of red, sable, and brindle. Black may or may not have tan or brindle points. White flashings are usual. Blue merle (black and gray, marbled) may or may not have tan or brindle points. Any other-than-specified body color or predominantly white are disqualifications. **Pembroke.** The Pembroke's colors are red, sable, fawn, black, and tan with or without white markings. White body color ("whitelies") or a distinct bluish or smoky cast to colored areas ("bluies") are very serious faults. The standard is very specific as to where white markings may and may not appear and white markings outside those perimeters are consid-

An excellent example of the Pembroke Welsh Corgi.

ered mismarks as are dogs who are black with white markings and no tan.

Character and Temperament: The differences in character and temperament of the two breeds are not made particularly apparent in the official standards. This is probably because they are not characteristics that are observable by sight. Although both Corgis are hard-working, intelligent herding dogs, extremely dedicated to those they love and highly trainable, there are some marked differences in the manner in which each of the breeds approaches life.

Those familiar with both breeds consider the Pembroke a bit bolder than its cousin, the Cardigan. The latter approaches life with a slightly more placid attitude.

According to the breed standard, the Pembroke Welsh Corgi's head "should be foxy in shape and appearance."

The Pembroke Corgi has of course far outdistanced the Cardigan in popularity and actually for little apparent reason. The late Mrs. Thelma Gray, considered the true doyen of both Corgis, felt a good part of the disparity could be due in part to the names of the two breeds. She is quoted in an article written for England's *Dog World* as saying, "I have always thought it was a very great pity that the two breeds were named as they have been. Had the Cardigan Welsh Corgi become known as Welsh Dogs or Welsh Heelers I believe that their unique and endearing characteristics would have carried them to fame in the world of dogs long since."

Disqualifications: Disqualifications are those flaws in a given dog that would bar it from competing in AKC shows. They are clearly identified in a breed's standard of excellence and are rigidly adhered to in conformation judging. To avoid perpetuating these faults the dogs possessing them should never be used for breeding. In most cases show ring disqualifications do not eliminate the possibility of the dog serving a happy healthy life as a companion.

The Pembroke Corgi: The Pembroke standard lists no official disqualifications.

The Cardigan Corgi: The standard of the Cardigan lists five disqualifications:
1. Blue eyes, or partially blue eyes, in any coat color other than blue merle.
2. Drop ears.
3. Nose other than solid black except in blue merles.
4. Any color other than specified.
5. Body color predominantly white.

The Cardigan (below) has a more prominent nose than the Pembroke, and large ears for its size.

OFFICIAL STANDARDS FOR WELSH CORGIS

Official Standard for the Pembroke Welsh Corgi

General Appearance—Low-set, strong, sturdily built and active, giving an impression of substance and stamina in a small space. Should not be so low and heavy-boned as to appear coarse or overdone, nor so light-boned as to appear racy. Outlook bold, but kindly. Expression intelligent and interested. Never shy nor vicious.

Correct type, including general balance and outline, attractiveness of headpiece, intelligent outlook and correct temperament is of primary importance. Movement is especially important, particularly as viewed from the side. A dog with smooth and free gait has to be reasonably sound and must be highly regarded. A minor fault must never take precedence over the above desired qualities.

A dog must be very seriously penalized for the following faults, regardless of whatever desirable qualities the dog may present: oversized or undersized; button, rose or drop ears; overshot or undershot bite; fluffies, whitelies, mismarks or bluies.

Size, Proportion, Substance—*Height* (from ground to highest point on withers) should be 10 to 12 inches. *Weight* is in proportion to size, not exceeding 30 pounds for dogs and 28 pounds for bitches. In show condition, the preferred medium sized dog of correct bone and substance will weigh approximately 27 pounds, with bitches approximately 25 pounds. Obvious oversized specimens and diminutive toylike individuals must be very severely penalized.

Proportions—Moderately long and low. The distance from the withers to the base of the tail should be approximately 40 percent greater than the distance from the withers to the ground. *Substance*—Should not be so low and heavy-boned as to appear coarse or overdone, nor so light-boned as to appear racy.

Head—The head should be foxy in shape and appearance. *Expression*—Intelligent and interested, but not sly. *Skull*—should be fairly wide and flat between the ears. Moderate amount of stop. Very slight rounding of cheek, not filled in below the eyes, as foreface should be nicely chiseled to give a somewhat tapered muzzle. Distance from occiput to center of stop to be greater than the distance from stop to nose tip, the proportion being five parts of total distance for the skull and three parts for the foreface. Muzzle should be neither dish-faced nor Roman-nosed. *Eyes*—oval, medium in size, not round, nor protruding, nor deepset and piglike. Set somewhat obliquely. Variations of brown in

harmony with coat color. Eye rims dark, preferably black. While dark eyes enhance the expression, true black eyes are most undesirable, as
are yellow or bluish eyes. *Ears*—Erect, firm, and
of medium size, tapering slightly to a rounded
point. Ears are mobile, and react sensitively to
sounds. A line drawn from the nose tip through
the eyes to the ear tips, and across, should form
an approximate equilateral triangle. Bat ears,
small catlike ears, overly large weak ears,
hooded ears, ears carried too high or too low,
are undesirable. Button, rose or drop ears are
very serious faults. *Nose*—Black and fully pig-
mented. *Mouth*— Scissors bite, the inner side of
the upper incisors touching the outer side of
the lower incisors. Level bite is acceptable.
Overshot or undershot bite is a very serious
fault. *Lips*—Black, tight with little or no fullness.

Neck, Topline, Body—*Neck*—Fairly long. Of
sufficient length to provide overall balance of
the dog. Slightly arched, clean and blending
well into the shoulders. A very short neck giving a stuffy appearance and a long, thin or ewe
neck are faulty. *Topline*—Firm and level, neither
riding up to nor falling away at the croup. A
slight depression behind the shoulders caused
by heavier neck coat meeting the shorter body
coat is permissible. *Body*—Rib cage should be
well sprung, slightly egg-shaped and moderately long. Deep chest, well let down between
the forelegs. Exaggerated lowness interferes
with the desired freedom of movement and
should be penalized. Viewed from above, the
body should taper slightly to end of loin. Loin
short. Round or flat rib cage, lack of brisket,
extreme length or cobbiness, are undesirable.
Tail—Docked as short as possible without being
indented. Occasionally a puppy is born with a
natural dock, which, if sufficiently short, is

acceptable. A tail up to two inches in length is
allowed, but if carried high tends to spoil the
contour of the topline.

Forequarters—*Legs*—Short forearms turned
slightly inward, with the distance between
wrists less than between the shoulder joints, so
that the front does not appear absolutely
straight. Ample bone carried right down into
the feet. Pasterns firm and nearly straight when
viewed from the side. Weak pasterns and
knuckling over are serious faults. Shoulder
blades long and well laid back along the rib
cage. Upper arms nearly equal in length to
shoulder blades. Elbows parallel to the body,
not prominent, and well set back to allow a line
perpendicular to the ground to be drawn from
tip of the shoulder blade through to elbow.
Feet—Oval, with the two center toes slightly in
advance of the two outer ones. Turning neither
in nor out. Pads strong and feet arched. Nails
short. Dewclaws on both forelegs and hindlegs
usually removed. Too round, long and narrow,
or splayed feet are faulty.

Hindquarters—Ample bone, strong and flexible, moderately angulated at stifle and hock.
Exaggerated angulation is as faulty as too little.
Thighs should be well muscled. Hocks short, parallel, and when viewed from the side are perpendicular to the ground. Barrel hocks or cowhocks
are most objectionable. Slipped or double jointed
hocks are very faulty. *Feet*—as in front.

Coat—Medium length; short, thick, weather
resistant undercoat with a coarser, longer outer
coat. Overall length varies, with slightly thicker
and longer ruff around the neck, chest and on
the shoulders. The body coat lies flat. Hair is
slightly longer on back of forelegs and underparts and somewhat fuller and longer on rear
of hindquarters. The coat is preferably straight,

but some waviness is permitted. This breed has a shedding coat, and seasonal lack of undercoat should not be too severely penalized, providing the hair is glossy, healthy and well groomed. A wiry, tightly marcelled coat is very faulty, as is an overly short, smooth and thin coat. *Very Serious Faults: Fluffies*—a coat of extreme length with exaggerated feathering on ears, chest, legs and feet, underparts and hindquarters. Trimming such a coat does not make it any more acceptable. The Corgi should be shown in its natural condition, with no trimming permitted except to tidy the feet, and, if desired, remove the whiskers.

Color—The outer coat is to be of self colors in red, sable, fawn, black and tan with or without white markings. White is acceptable on legs, chest, neck (either in part or as a collar), muzzle, underparts and as a narrow blaze on head. *Very Serious Faults: Whitelies*—Body color white, with red or dark markings. *Bluies*—Colored portions of the coat have a distinct bluish or smoky cast. This coloring is associated with extremely light or blue eyes, liver or gray eye rims, nose and lip pigment. *Mismarks*—Self colors with any area of white on the back between withers and tail, on sides between elbows and back of hindquarters, or on ears. Black with white markings and no tan present.

Gait—Free and smooth. Forelegs should reach well forward without too much lift, in unison with the driving action of the hind legs. The correct shoulder assembly and well-fitted elbows allow a long, free stride in front. Viewed from the front, legs do not move in exact parallel planes, but incline slightly inward to compensate for shortness of leg and width of chest. Hind legs should drive well under the body and move on a line with the forelegs,

with hocks turning neither in nor out. Feet must travel parallel to the line of motion with no tendency to swing out, cross over or interfere with each other. Short, choppy movement, rolling or high-stepping gait, close or overly wide coming or going, are incorrect. This is a herding dog, which must have the agility, freedom of movement, and endurance to do the work for which he was developed.

Temperament—Outlook bold, but kindly. Never shy or vicious. The judge shall dismiss from the ring any Pembroke Welsh Corgi that is excessively shy.

Approved June 13, 1972
Reformatted January 28, 1993

Official Standard for the Cardigan Welsh Corgi

General Appearance—Low set with moderately heavy bone and deep chest. Overall silhouette long in proportion to height, culminating in a low tail set and fox-like brush. *General Impression*—A handsome, powerful, small dog, capable of both speed and endurance, intelligent, sturdily built but not coarse.

Size, Proportion, Substance—Overall balance is more important than absolute size. Dogs and bitches should be from 10.5 to 12.5 inches at the withers when standing naturally. The ideal length/height ratio is 1.8:1 when measuring from the point of the breast bone (prosternum) to the rear of the hip (ischial tuberosity) and measuring from the ground to the point of the withers. Ideally, dogs should be from 30 to 38 pounds; bitches from 25 to 34 pounds. Lack of overall balance, oversized or undersized are *serious faults*.

Head—The *head* should be refined in accordance with the sex and substance of the dog. It should never appear so large and heavy nor so small and fine as to be out of balance with the rest of the dog. *Expression* alert and gentle, watchful, yet friendly. *Eyes* medium to large, not bulging, with dark rims and distinct corners. Widely set. Clear and dark in harmony with coat color. Blue eyes (including partially blue eyes), or one dark and one blue eye permissible in blue merles, and in any other coat color than blue merle are a *disqualification*. *Ears* large and prominent in proportion to size of dog. Slightly rounded at the tip, and of good strong leather. Moderately wide at the

The standard of the Cardigan Welsh Corgi defines a dog that is "low set with moderately heavy bone and (has a) deep chest." The standard also describes the overall silhouette as "long in proportion to height" and "culminating in a low tail set and fox-like brush."

base, carried erect and sloping slightly forward when alert. When erect, tips are slightly wide of a straight line drawn from the tip of the nose through the center of the eye. Small and/or pointed ears are *serious faults*. Drop ears are a *disqualification*.

The Pembroke ranks 37th among the 146 breeds the AKC registers.

Skull—Top moderately wide and flat between the ears, showing no prominence of occiput, tapering towards the eyes. Slight depression between the eyes. *Cheeks* flat with some chiseling where the cheek meets the foreface and under the eye. There should be no prominence of cheekbone. *Muzzle* from the tip of the nose to the base of the stop should be shorter than the length of the skull from the base of the stop to the high point of the occiput, the proportion

The Cardigan Corgi's expression should be "alert and gentle, watchful, yet friendly," if it is to meet the requirements of the breed standard.

being about three parts muzzle to five parts skull: rounded but not blunt; tapered but not pointed. In profile the plane of the muzzle should parallel that of the skull, but on a lower level due to a definite but moderate *stop*. *Nose* black, except in blue merles where black noses are preferred but butterfly noses are tolerated. A nose other than solid black in any other color is a *disqualification. Lips* fit cleanly and evenly together all around. *Jaws* strong and clean. Underjaw moderately deep and well formed, reaching to the base of the nose and rounded at the chin. *Teeth* strong and regular. Scissors bite preferred; i.e., inner side of upper incisors fitting closely over outer side of lower incisors. Overshot, undershot, or wry bite are *serious faults.*

Neck, Topline, Body—*Neck* moderately long and muscular without throatiness. Well developed, especially in males, and in proportion to the dog's build. Neck well set on; fits into strong, well shaped shoulders. *Topline* level. *Body* long and strong. *Chest* moderately broad with prominent breastbone. Deep brisket, with well sprung ribs to allow for good lungs. Ribs extending well back. *Loin* short, strong, moderately tucked up. Waist well defined.

Croup—Slight downward slope to the tail set.

Tail set fairly low on body line and reaching well below hock. Carried low when standing or moving slowly, streaming out parallel to ground when at a dead run, lifted when excited, but never curled over the back. High tail set is a *serious fault.*

Forequarters—The moderately broad chest tapers to a deep brisket, well let down between the forelegs. *Shoulders* slope downward and outward from the withers sufficiently to accommodate desired rib-spring. Shoulder blade (scapula) long and well laid back, meeting upper arm (humerus) at close to a right angle. Humerus nearly as long as scapula. *Elbows* should fit close, being neither loose nor tied. The *forearms* (ulna and radius) should be curved to fit spring of ribs. The curve in the forearm makes the wrists (carpal joints) somewhat closer together than the elbows. The *pasterns* are strong and flexible. Dewclaws removed.

The *feet* are relatively large and rounded, with well filled pads. They point slightly outward from a straight-ahead position to balance the width of the shoulders. This outward point is not to be more than 30 degrees from center line when viewed from above. The toes should not be splayed.

The correct Cardigan front is neither straight nor so crooked as to appear unsound. Overall, the bone should be heavy for a dog of this size, but not so heavy as to appear coarse or reduce agility. Knuckling over, straight front, fiddle front are *serious faults.*

Hindquarters—Well muscled and strong, but slightly less wide than shoulders. Hipbone (pelvis) slopes downward with the croup, forming a right angle with the femur at the hip socket. There should be moderate angulation at stifle and hock. Hocks well let down. Metatarsi perpendicular to the ground and parallel to each other. Dewclaws removed. *Feet* point straight ahead and are slightly smaller and more oval than front. Toes arched. Pads well filled. Overall, the hindquarters must denote sufficient power to propel this low, relatively heavy herding dog efficiently over rough terrain.

Coat—Medium length but dense as it is double. Outer hairs slightly harsh in texture; never wiry, curly or silky. Lies relatively smooth and is weather resistant. The insulating undercoat is short, soft and thick. A correct coat has short hair on ears, head, the legs; medium hair on body; and slightly longer, thicker hair in ruff, on the backs of the thighs to form "pants," and on the underside of the tail. The coat should not be so exaggerated as to appear fluffy. This breed has a shedding coat, and seasonal lack of undercoat should not be too severely penalized, providing the hair is healthy. Trimming is not allowed except to tidy feet and, if desired, remove whiskers. Soft guard hairs, uniform length, wiry, curly, silky, overly short and/or flat coats are not desired. A distinctly long or fluffy coat is an extremely *serious fault.*

Color—All shades of red, sable and brindle. Black with or without tan or brindle points. Blue merle (black and gray; marbled) with or without tan or brindle points. There is no color preference. White flashings are usual on the neck (either in part or as a collar), chest, legs, muzzle, underparts, tip of tail and as a blaze on head. White on the head should not predominate and should never surround the eyes. Any color other than specified and/or body color predominantly white are *disqualifications.*

Gait—free and smooth. Effortless. Viewed from the side, forelegs should reach well forward when moving at a trot, without much lift, in unison with driving action of hind legs. The correct shoulder assembly and well fitted elbows allow for a long free stride in front.

Viewed from the front, legs do not move in exact parallel planes, but incline slightly inward to compensate for shortness of leg and width of chest. Hind legs, when trotting, should reach well under body, move on a line with the forelegs, with the hocks turning neither in nor out, and in one continuous motion drive powerfully behind, well beyond the set of the tail. Feet must travel parallel to the line of motion with no tendency to wing out, cross over, or interfere with each other. Short choppy movement, rolling or high-stepping gait, close or overly wide coming or going, are incorrect. This is a herding dog which must have the agility, freedom of movement, and endurance to do the work for which he was developed.

Temperament—Even-tempered, loyal, affectionate, and adaptable. Never shy nor vicious.

Disqualifications

Blue eyes, or partially blue eyes, in any coat color other than blue merle.

Drop ears.

Nose other than solid black except in blue merles.

Any color other than specified.

Body color predominantly white.

Approved December 13, 1994
Effective January 31, 1995

UNDERSTANDING THE CORGI

People find the two Corgi breeds attractive for many reasons. Both Corgis have big dog personalities in a moderate-sized package ideal for the average household. Others are attracted to the Corgi's intelligence and ability to understand its owner. Even after someone has decided which of the two Corgis he or she prefers, there is a wide range of colors and markings to choose from. While these are but a few of the valid assets of the Corgi, they are still not enough reason for anyone to rush out to buy a Corgi.

Neither of the Corgis is a breed that can be put outdoors in a pen and attended to only when the owner has the time or notion to do so. Corgis can be great companions and close friends for their entire lifespan, but only if their owner is ready to invest the time and patience required to bring the breed to its full potential.

Just about all puppies are cuddly and cute, with the little one-ear-up-and-one-ear-down Corgi pups especially so. This is the reason puppies are the subject of calendars and greeting cards printed around the world each year. It is important to realize, however, that a puppy will spend only a very small part of its day sitting around looking cute. The far greater part

of the day and night the puppy will spend investigating, digging, chewing, eating, relieving itself, needing to go outdoors, and then immediately insisting that it be let in. All too often these needs are not realistically considered before adding a dog to one's household.

The list of the real needs of any young puppy or an adult dog can be overwhelming to someone who has never owned a dog before. It takes time and planning to fulfill the day-to-day needs of a puppy or even a fully grown dog. This says nothing of the time required for the many lessons little Winston must be taught by his master before he understands what he may and may not do. The bottom line is that your puppy or dog will completely depend on you for everything it needs.

Friends often seek our advice when they are contemplating the purchase of their first dog. If we detect even the slightest uncertainty on their part, we always advise them to wait until they are absolutely sure they want to take on this great responsibility. Owning a dog requires a great commitment and it is not something that should ever be done on a whim. The hasty purchase of a dog can result in sheer drudgery and frustration for the owner, and an unhappy situation for the dog itself.

Failure to understand the amount of time and consideration a well-cared-for dog requires is one of the primary reasons for the number of unwanted canines that end their lives in an animal shelter. Given proper consideration beforehand, the purchase of a dog can bring many years of companionship and comfort as well as unconditional love and devotion no other animal can match.

The Good Dog Owner Test

Consider three very important questions:

1. Does the person who will ultimately be responsible for the dog's day-to-day care really want a dog?

In many active families the woman of the household is the person who will have the ultimate responsibility for the family dog. This appears to be the case even when the mother of the family works outside the home. She may not want any more duties than she already has. Pet care can be an excellent way to teach children responsibility, but beware—in their enthusiasm to have a puppy, children are apt to promise almost anything. It is what will happen after the novelty of owning a new dog has worn off that must be considered.

2. Does the lifestyle and schedule of the household lend itself to the demands of proper dog care?

There must always be someone available to see to a dog's basic needs: feeding, exercise, coat care, access to the outdoors when required, and so on. If you or the members of your family are gone from morning to night or if you travel frequently and are away from home for long periods of time, the dog still must be cared for. Will someone willingly be present to do so? Are you prepared to pay the costs of frequent boarding kennel housing for your dog while you are gone?

3. Is the kind of dog you are considering suitable for the individual or household?

Very young children can be very rough and unintentionally hurt a puppy of a small and fragile breed. Even puppies of the larger, sturdier breeds cannot tolerate being dropped or excessively rough treatment.

On the other hand, a young dog of a very large or very rambunctious breed can overwhelm and sometimes injure an infant or small child in an enthusiastic moment. Sharing a tiny apartment with very large breeds can prove extremely difficult for both dog and owner.

Toy breeds will have difficulty surviving northern winters if required to live outdoors in unheated quarters. A long-haired dog, while attractive, is hardly suitable for the individual who spends a great deal of time camping, hunting, or hiking through the woods.

In addition to the above three major questions regarding dog ownership, the prospective dog owner should strongly consider the specific peculiarities of his or her own lifestyle or household. All this applies whether the household is made up of a single individual or a large family. Everyone involved must realize that the new dog will not understand the household routine and must be taught *everything* you want it to know and do. This takes time and patience and often the most important lessons for the new dog to learn will take the longest for it to absorb.

If you were able to answer yes to all three of the questions in the "Good Dog Owner Test," move on to the following.

Purebred or Mongrel?

There is no difference in the love, devotion, and companionship that a mixed-breed dog and a purebred dog can give its owner. There are, however, some aspects of suitability that can best be fulfilled by the purebred dog.

Not all puppies will grow up to be particularly attractive adults or they may appeal only to someone with very exotic tastes. Predicting what a mixed-breed puppy will look like at maturity is almost impossible. Size, length of hair, and temperament can change drastically between puppyhood and adulthood and may not be at all what the owner had hoped. Then what happens to the dog?

In buying a purebred puppy, the purchaser will have a very good idea of what the dog will look like and how it will behave as an adult; purebred dogs have been bred for generations to meet specifications of conformation and temperament.

When choosing a puppy, one must have the adult dog in mind because the little fellow is going to be an adult much longer than it ever was a puppy. The adult dog is what must fit the owner's lifestyle and esthetic standards.

A fastidious housekeeper may well have second thoughts when trying to accommodate a very large breed that slobbers or one that sheds its coat all year round. Joggers or long-distance runners who want a dog to accompany them are not going to be happy with a short-legged or slow breed. It is also important to know that short-muzzled dogs and those with brachycephalic or "pushed-in" faces like the Pekingese, Pug, and Bulldog have very little heat tolerance. Consider these points *before* you select a puppy.

Since the conformation of purebred dogs is entirely predictable, the owner of a purebred puppy will know that the breed he or she selects will still be appropriate as an adult. Temperament in purebred dogs has great predictability, although there may be minor variations within a breed. The hair-trigger response and hyperactivity of certain breeds would not be at all suitable for someone who wants a quiet, contented companion, nor would the placid attitude of other breeds be desirable for someone who wants an athletic, exuberant dog to frolic with. With purebred dogs, you are reasonably assured of selecting a dog compatible with your lifestyle.

Price

The initial purchase price of a purebred dog could easily be a significant investment for the owner, but a purebred dog costs no more to maintain than a mixed breed. If the cost of having exactly the kind of dog you want and are proud to own is amortized over the number of years you will enjoy it, you will have to admit the initial cost becomes far less consequential.

Appearance

Before hastily buying a breed of dog whose *appearance* you find appealing, spend time with adult members of the breed or do some good research to assure yourself that you and the breed in question are temperamentally compatible. Visit kennels or breeders specializing in the breed of your choice. If you have not made up your mind as to which of the two Corgis you might like to have, visit kennels specializing in both breeds and spend some time with adult dogs. This should help you enormously in deciding if you are considering the right dog for you.

Your Best Friend?

Corgis are entirely capable of being man's (or woman's!) best friend but as is the case in any good relationship, both parties must be compatible. Corgis were bred to work. At no time in either breed's developmental history was any attempt made to make the Corgi a lapdog or boudoir companion. A Corgi best belongs to someone who will not begrudge the time it takes to give the dog a job. Corgis must have something to do or they may well use up their excess time by inventing things to do. Unfortunately, what your Corgi decides is "something to do" might be gnawing one of the legs off your best antique table, excavating your newly planted flower bed, or herding your children.

Retrieving comes naturally to Corgis and putting the talent to use in bringing you the morning paper or in some cleverly devised game is "work" your dog will enjoy. Although obedience work might mean one thing to you, to a Corgi it could mean the difference between boredom and a job that it looks forward to performing well.

All this is not to indicate your Corgi is an incessantly busy or neurotic little pet. On the contrary, your dog will enjoy those quiet moments sitting next to you while you read or listen to music as much as you do. However, your Corgi needs directed activity to take the edge off its inherited ability to put in a full day's work. Corgis are lovers of routine and once they learn the household routine they are usually one step ahead of their owners in following it.

Do not mistake routine for taking a Corgi's patience to its limits. Approach training your Corgi with variety and enthusiasm. Repeating a lesson over and over will bore the average Corgi and it will rebel, some Corgi owners say, "just to put a slightly different slant on what it is doing!"

Deciding Who Is Boss

This is definitely a breed with a highly developed sense of curiosity and a mind of its own. If a Corgi is

The buyer will have a very good idea of what the little Corgi puppy will grow up to look like—and a handsome package it will be!

involved in exploring or in tracking down some real or imagined mystery creature, answering your first call may not be nearly as enticing.

Owners who have been negligent in making their Corgi understand who makes all the rules may find themselves left out of decision making entirely. If you do not provide that leadership, Dutchess will find herself entirely capable of providing that leadership for herself.

With all that said, if a prospective owner is willing to take on the responsibilities required of a responsible Corgi owner, there are few breeds that can provide more devotion and companionship than this one. Corgis live to be with their owners and are able to do that since they are just about the right size to go anywhere—not too large and not too small, short of coat and long on endurance, tolerant of both heat and cold. Corgis love their homes and have no great urge to roam, especially if there is plenty to do at home; however, they are curious and lacking a

All puppies are adorable—practically irresistible. Corgi puppies are no exception, but they grow up to be busy, active adults needing owners who are willing to supply all their requirements.

fenced yard a Corgi might decide it should check out the other side of the mountain on occasion.

Corgis can be trained to do just about anything a dog is capable of doing, particularly if the task includes agility and enthusiasm. The only thing Corgis are short on is their legs. Children quickly earn the breed's devotion and protection without trying.

Male or Female?

While some people may have their personal preferences as to the sex of their dog, we can honestly say that both the male and the female

Corgi make equally good companions and are equal in their trainability and affection. The decision will have more to do with the lifestyle and ultimate plans of the owner than differences between the sexes in the breed.

On the other hand, as experienced owners of at least two alpha-type female Pembroke Corgis, we can offer one bit of advice. Whatever applies to making a Corgi understand who is in charge is especially true of some Pembroke Corgi females. As sweet and affectionate as they can be, some females can also develop a stubborn streak a mile wide. "Determined" can be an understatement when describing some of the lady Pembrokes we've known. These young ladies are bright enough to know who they can challenge and who not to even attempt to hoodwink.

Once these bossy females have learned that it is *possible* to get away with something, it will be extremely hard to change their minds. This does not necessarily apply to *all* female Pembroke Corgis but occurs often enough so that it is worth mentioning.

Males of both Corgi breeds, however, tend to be what could be referred to as "pushovers." They are good old boys who seem to go along with pretty much everything their loved ones desire. It takes them a bit longer to grow up than it does their sisters, but the boys are usually most cooperative.

The male Corgi is normally larger and heavier boned than the female and does present one problem that the prospective buyer should consider. While both the male and the female must be trained not to urinate in the home, the male of any breed of dog has a natural instinct to lift his leg and urinate on objects to establish and "mark" his territory. The degree of effort that must be invested in training the male not to do this varies with the individual dog. This habit becomes increasingly more difficult to correct with the number of times a male dog is used for breeding; the mating act increases his need and desire to mark his territory.

The female is not entirely problem-free. She will have her semiannual, and sometimes burdensome, heat cycle after she is eight or nine months old. At these times she must be confined so that she will not soil her surroundings, and she must also be closely watched to prevent male dogs from gaining access to her or she will become pregnant.

Altering

Both of these sexually associated problems can be effectively eliminated by having your pet Corgi "altered" (see Spaying and Neutering, page 65). Spaying the female and neutering the male will not change the personality of your pet and will avoid many problems. Neutering the male Corgi can reduce his aggressive attitude toward other males and will reduce, if not entirely eliminate, his desire to pursue a neighborhood female that shows signs of an impending romantic attitude.

Neutering and spaying also preclude the possibility of your pet adding to the pet overpopulation problem that concerns environmentalists worldwide. Altering also reduces the risk of mammary cancer in the female and testicular cancer in the male.

It is important to understand, however, that these are not reversible procedures. If you are considering the possibility of showing your Corgi, be aware that altered animals are not allowed to compete in American Kennel Club or United Kennel Club conformation dog shows. Altered dogs may, however, compete in herding and obedience trials, agility events, and field trials.

Where to Buy Your Corgi

Your Corgi will live with you for many years. The two Corgi breeds regularly enjoy long, healthy lives, easily living to be twelve, fourteen, very often fifteen or sixteen years of age. It is extremely important, therefore, that the dog come from a source where physical and mental soundness are primary considerations in the breeding program, usually the result of careful breeding over a period of many years. Selective breeding is aimed at maintaining the virtues of the breed and eliminating genetic weaknesses. Because this selective breeding is time-consuming and costly, good breeders protect their investment by providing the best prenatal care for their breeding females and nutrition for the growing puppies. There is no substitute for the amount of dedication and care good breeders give their dogs.

The Pembroke Welsh Corgi Club of America, The Cardigan Welsh Corgi Club of America, and both the American Kennel Club and the United Kennel Club (see Information, page 124) can provide the prospective buyer with the names and addresses of responsible individuals who have intelligently bred Corgis available for sale. Often, veterinarians can refer you directly to them as well.

Breeders—What to Consider

There is a good chance that there are reputable Pembroke Corgi breeders located nearby who will not only be able to provide the dog you are looking for but who will be able to advise you regularly in proper care and feeding.

There may be a bit more of a problem in locating a Cardigan Corgi breeder as the breed is numerically small and Cardigan breeders do not breed often. They often have long waiting lists for the puppies that are available. Those who own Cardigans, however, feel the breed is well worth the wait and can refer you to good breeders.

Visiting a breeder's home or kennel gives the buyer the distinct advantage of seeing the parents, or at least the mother, of the puppies that are available. They normally have other relatives of the dog you are interested in on the premises as well. The majority of these breeders will be more than happy to show you their dogs and to discuss the advantages and responsibilities involved in owning the breed. Responsible breeders are as concerned about their stock being placed in the right hands as the prospective buyer is in obtaining a sound and healthy dog.

SELECTING A CORGI PUPPY

Visiting the Breeder

On your first visit, do not hesitate to ask questions and to ask to see the breeder's mature dogs. While Corgis, generally speaking, are long-lived hardy dogs, there are a few hereditary defects that occur. Experienced breeders know which hereditary problems exist in the breed and will be happy to discuss them with you. Practically all breeds are subject to inherited ailments and Corgis are no exception.

Beware of breeders who tell you that their dogs are not susceptible to inherited diseases or potential problems. We do not mean to imply that all Corgis are afflicted with genetic problems, but a reliable breeder will give you the information you are entitled to know regarding the individual you are considering. Refer to Inherited Health Problems and Diseases, beginning on page 92, for details on some of the genetic ailments that might exist in Corgis.

Most reliable breeders provide certificates documenting that the puppies they are selling are free of the breed's genetic problems. There are some tests that cannot be completed until the dog is close to adulthood, but even in cases such as these, documentation that the parents of the puppy have been tested are usually available.

Temperament and health of the parents of your prospective purchase are extremely important. Do see the parents, or at the very least, the mother, of your prospective purchase.

If you dislike what you observe in any of the dogs related to your puppy, *look elsewhere!*

Environment

Inspect the environment in which the dogs are raised. Cleanliness is as important to producing good stock as are good pedigrees. The time you spend in researching and inspecting the kennel and the adult dogs it houses may well save you a great deal of money and heartache in the years to come.

All this is not to imply your Corgi puppy must come from a large kennel. On the contrary, today many good puppies are produced by small hobby breeders in their homes. There will probably be as many small breeders included in recommendations from the Corgi parent clubs and the United and American Kennel Clubs as there are large professional kennels. These individuals offer the same investment of time, study, and knowledge as the larger kennels and they are just as ready to offer the same health guarantees. An added advantage of buying a puppy from one of these small breeders is that they often have a great deal more time to devote to socializing their puppies and the puppies are raised in a family atmosphere.

A newspaper advertisement may or may not lead you to a reputable hobby breeder. It is up to you to investigate and compare as you would in the case of any major purchase. Good hobby breeders will sell only to approved buyers and they spend considerable time in determining this. If the seller is willing to let you make a purchase with no questions asked, you should be highly suspicious. Reliable breeders ask the prospective purchaser many questions not only to satisfy themselves the puppy will be going into a good home, but also to help them determine which puppy from a litter might be most suitable for the buyer.

Knowing your likes and dislikes and how the dog will become a part of your life may determine one puppy might be better for you than another. There are both aggressive and more passive puppies in every litter. Knowing a bit about your lifestyle and your expectations for the Corgi you buy will help the seller make the right match.

Finally, a good question to ask the breeder of the puppy you are considering is "why" he or she breeds Corgis. A responsible breeder will have definite reasons for having produced a litter. The reasons could be varied because the Corgi is a very adaptable breed suitable for many purposes but if you suspect the breeder you are speaking to breeds only to sell puppies, we would suggest you look elsewhere.

Deciding on Which One

After you have settled in your mind which of the two Corgis is the dog for you and then where your puppy will be coming from, you will immediately be faced with that often difficult decision as to which of the puppies available in a litter would be best for you.

Do take a breeder's recommendations seriously. The breeder has lived with the puppies since their birth and is in tune with the little idiosyncrasies of each of them. You and your puppy will be living together for a long time, so the better matched your personalities are, the more fruitful your relationship will be.

Above all, the Corgi puppy you buy should be a happy, playful extrovert. Never select a puppy that appears sickly because you feel sorry for it and feel you will be able to nurse it back to good health. Well-bred Corgi puppies with positive temperaments are not afraid of strangers. The AKC standards of both Corgis are very specific in their requirement of sound and stable temperaments; you should not settle for anything less. Under normal circumstances you will have the whole litter in your lap if you kneel and call them to you.

If one puppy in particular appeals to you, pick it up and ask the breeder if you can spend some time alone with the pup. As long as a puppy is still in a fairly familiar environment where scents and sounds are not entirely strange, it should remain relaxed and happy in your arms. Avoid the puppy that becomes tense and struggles to escape.

Physical Signs

When you and your prospective puppy are alone, you will have an opportunity to examine the puppy more closely:

◆ Check inside the puppy's ears. They should be pink and clean. Any odor or dark discharge could indicate ear mites, which in turn would indicate poor maintenance.

◆ The inside of the puppy's mouth and gums should be pink; the teeth should be clean and white. There should be no malformation of the mouth or jaw.

◆ The eyes should be clear and bright. Again, be aware of any signs of discharge.

◆ Corgi puppies should feel compact and substantial to the touch, never bony and undernourished; nor should they be bloated: a taut and bloated abdomen is usually a sign of worms; a rounded puppy belly is normal.

◆ The nose of a Corgi puppy should never be crusted or running.

◆ Coughing or signs of diarrhea are danger signals as are skin eruptions.

◆ Conformation is important even at an early age. The movement should be free and easy. Limping or stumbling could easily mean lifelong problems.

If you have been reading and doing your research, you can expect the Corgi puppy to look much like a miniaturized version of an adult. The puppy coat will be softer and finer but the hair should never be long or fluffy. Ears may not yet be standing or one ear may be up and the other down. If the ears aren't standing, simply hold the puppy on its back in your two hands and tilt its head downward. The ears will lie back and this will give you a picture of what the puppy will look like when the ears stand on their own. Ears may seem a bit large at this early stage, but more often than not the puppy will grow into them. All in all, the baby Corgi does not go through the extreme metamorphosis that some other breeds do.

Raising a Puppy

Raising a puppy is a wonderful experience; granted, at times it can also be one of the most exasperating experiences you have ever attempted. In the end, though, having endured each other through all the trials of puppyhood, you and your Corgi will forge a bond that has no equal.

Should you decide that you do, in fact, wish to raise this little Corgi tyke from infancy to adulthood, be aware that most breeders do not—and should not—release their puppies until they have had their initial inoculations. This usually takes place at about eight to ten weeks of age, although some breeders are now opting to wait a bit longer. While they are still nursing, puppies receive a degree of temporary immunity to diseases through their mother. Once they have been weaned, they lose this immunity and must be appropriately inoculated. It is wise not to remove a puppy from its home before the breeder has given it all vaccinations appropriate for its age.

Prior to immunization, puppies are very susceptible to infectious diseases. Many such diseases may be transmitted via the clothing and hands of people. After the appropriate series of vaccinations the breeder will inform you when your Corgi puppy is ready to leave its first home.

Show Dog or Companion?

If you want to be assured of a dog of real show quality, then the fact that the puppy comes from winning stock becomes a major consideration. Also, the older the puppy is at the time of selection, the more likely you will know how good a dog you will have at maturity. The most any breeder can say about an eight-week-old Corgi puppy is that it has or does not have "show potential."

If you are seriously interested in having a Corgi puppy of the quality to show or to breed, wait with your selection until the puppy is at least five to six months old. By this time, you can be far more certain of dentition, soundness, and attitude, as well as other important

Deciding on which puppy is the right one for you can present quite a problem.

characteristics. No matter what you have in mind for your dog's future—obedience trials, dog shows, herding or agility trials, or nothing more than loving companionship—all of the foregoing should be considered carefully and, above all, temperament of the puppy and of its parents must be a paramount factor in deciding which Corgi to take home.

If the excitement and pride of owning a winning show dog appeals to you, we strongly urge you to seek out a successful breeder who has a record of having produced winning dogs through the years. As stated, it is extremely difficult, if not impossible, to predict what an eight-week-old puppy will look like as an adult. An experienced breeder, however, will know whether a young puppy has "potential." Unfortunately, many prospective owners who want a show dog also want a very young puppy and at the same time they want some guarantee that the puppy will grow up to be a winner at maturity. It is not possible to give that kind of guarantee, and no honest breeder will do so. The breeder may agree to replace the puppy with another if it does not turn out to be a show dog but this also usually entails returning the grown puppy to the breeder. Most people have become too attached to the dog they have raised to consider doing that.

Show-prospect Puppies

A show-prospect puppy must not only meet all the health and soundness qualifications of the good pet puppy, it must show every sign that it will conform very closely to the rigid demands of the breed standard (see page 19) when it matures. It might make little difference to you if your pet's coat is much longer than the ideal or that a male has only one testicle, but faults like this make a great deal of difference in determining the future of a show dog. Cosmetic faults are usually of little concern to the owner who does not plan to show or breed and who will undoubtedly have the dog sexually altered anyway.

We have known some people who have spent thousands of dollars buying very young puppies again and again but have never achieved their goal of owning a winning show dog. Granted, an older puppy or grown dog may initially cost considerably more than an eight-week-old puppy, but odds are much greater that in the end you will have what you actually wanted.

Experienced and successful Corgi breeders have spent years developing a line of top-quality animals. These breeders know what to look for in the breed and they are particularly familiar with the manner in which their own stock matures.

After you have decided which of the two Corgi breeds is the right one for you, your next step is to visit kennels that have a reputation for breeding healthy dogs with good temperaments.

If one puppy in particular appeals to you, pick it up and ask the breeder if you can take it into another room away from its littermates. Avoid the puppy that struggles to escape.

Price of a Puppy

The price of a Corgi puppy can vary considerably but it should be understood that reputable breeders have invested considerable time, skill, and work in making sure they have the best possible breeding stock, all of which costs a great deal of money. Good breeders have also invested substantially in veterinary supervision and testing to keep their stock as free from hereditary defects as possible.

A puppy purchased from an established and successful breeder may cost a few more dollars initially, but the small additional investment can save many trips to the veterinarian over the ensuing years. It is heartbreaking to become attached to a dog only to lose it at an early age because of some health defect.

You should expect to pay $500 or more for an eight-week-old, pet-quality Corgi puppy. Older puppies will cost more. Youngsters with show and breeding potential may be double that price and young show stock that has reached the five- or six-month-old stage will be even more expensive. It is wise to remember, however, that purchasing a puppy is like anything else in life—you get what you pay for.

Veterinary Health Check

Responsible Corgi breeders are always willing to supply a written agreement that the sale of a puppy is contingent upon the puppy's successfully passing a veterinary health check. If the location of the breeder, your home, and your prospective veterinarian allow it, plan the time of day you pick up your puppy so that you can go directly from the breeder to the veterinarian. If this is not possible, you should plan the visit as soon as possible. No longer

than 24 hours should elapse before this is done.

Carry your puppy when you are going into and out of your veterinarian's office. A good idea is to have the puppy in a carrying case and keep the puppy in the crate while you are waiting for the veterinarian to see you. Veterinary hospitals have many sick dogs coming and going all day long; you do not want your vulnerable puppy to come in contact with the places these sick dogs have sat or walked.

Should the puppy not pass the veterinary health check, a responsible and ethical breeder will be more than happy either to refund your money or provide you with another puppy depending on the stipulations of the contract.

Necessary Documents

Inoculations and Health Certificates

By the time your Corgi puppy is ready to leave its littermates it will undoubtedly have been vaccinated against hepatitis, leptospirosis, distemper, parainfluenza, and canine parvovirus. Rabies inoculations are usually not given until the puppy is six months of age. There is a set series of inoculations developed to combat these and other infectious diseases and more details are given in the chapter Accidents and Illnesses, beginning on page 87.

You are entitled to have a record of these inoculations when you purchase your puppy. Most breeders will give you complete documentation, along with dates on which your puppy was wormed and examined by the veterinarian. Usually, this record will also indicate when booster shots are required. These are very important records to keep safe; they will be needed by the veterinarian you select to care for your Corgi.

Pedigree and Registration Certificate

Buying a purebred dog also entitles you to a copy of the dog's pedigree and registration certificate. These are two separate documents. The former is simply the dog's family tree and lists the registered names of your Corgi's sire and dam along with their ancestors usually for at least four generations.

Official registration certificates are issued by the major purebred dog organization of every country. In the United States registrations are issued either by the American Kennel Club or the United Kennel Club, the two major purebred dog organizations.

When ownership of your Corgi is transferred from the breeder's name to your name, the transaction is entered on this certificate, and, once mailed to the appropriate organization, it is permanently recorded in their computerized records. You are then sent a copy of the duly recorded change. File this document in a safe place along with your other important papers, as you will need it should you ever wish to show or breed your Corgi.

It is important to understand that a pedigree is simply a listing of the dog's ancestors. The fact that a dog has a pedigree means nothing more than that it is purebred, that all its ancestors, in fact, are either Pembroke or Cardigan Corgis, respectively. The pedigree does not mean a Corgi is of superior or show quality. All of the dogs in the pedigree could have been of strictly pet quality. On the other hand, the pedigree could just as well be made up of Corgis that have won many show ring titles. Usu-

ally dogs that have won their championships are printed in red on a pedigree.

Diet Sheet

A sound and healthy Corgi puppy is in that condition because it has been properly fed and cared for. Every breeder has a slightly different approach to successful nutrition, so it is wise to obtain a written record or description that details the amount and kind of food your puppy has been receiving. It should also indicate the number of times a day your puppy has been accustomed to being fed and the kind of vitamin supplementation, if any, it has been receiving.

Maintaining this program for at least the first week or two after your puppy comes home with you will reduce the chances of digestive upsets and loose stools. When and if changes are made, they should be made gradually. A good diet program will also project increases in food and the appropriate changes that should be made in the dog's diet as it matures.

How About an Adult Dog?

A young puppy is not your only option in choosing a Corgi to come and live with you. For some people, especially the elderly, a house-trained adult can be an excellent choice. Also, if time available to house-train is limited, or the owner expects to be away from home frequently, an adult Corgi can be a wise choice.

Often, breeders will have young adult Corgis that were held back in hope they would develop into dogs worthy of becoming show champions. Just as often the youngsters do not live up to those expectations but would nevertheless be wonderful companions.

The inside of a puppy's mouth and gums should be pink and the teeth should be clean white. There should be no malformation of the mouth or jaw.

on having their own family to love and care for and they can make ideal pets.

If, in fact, your Corgi will be a working Corgi—one you plan to use on livestock—a young adult or even one fully matured that has been trained may be just the answer. A trained Corgi knows what it has been taught and will perform well for a new owner so long as the new owner has learned how to give commands properly.

Practically all Corgis, even adults, seem to adapt to their new environments very easily.

This cannot be said for all other breeds. The mature Corgi also needs far less supervision than a puppy, because it has normally passed through the mischievous stage and the need to chew. Usually, an adult Corgi is ready, willing, and capable of learning the household routine.

On the other hand, the adult dog that was raised in a kennel may have developed habits that you do not find acceptable. Kennel dogs are not always house-trained and may have great difficulty trying to understand this concept after reaching adulthood. In some cases it may be difficult to retrain such animals.

Until you begin to work together, there is no way of knowing how willing an adult Corgi is to learn new habits. Always take an adult dog home on a trial basis to see how it works out

Also, there are occasions in which a breeder may be willing to place an entirely mature Corgi that they no longer wish to use for breeding and prefer that it have the advantage of living in a one-family home rather than spending the rest of its life as a kennel dog. These "grown-up" Corgis always seem to thrive

Raising a Corgi through all the trials of puppyhood can forge a bond that has few equals. This happy little Cardigan will make someone a wonderful lifetime companion.

Experienced and successful breeders have a better chance of anticipating the general direction maturity will take their show-prospect puppies.

for both you and the dog. In the first place, most breeders will only agree to placing an adult Corgi on a trial basis and the buyer must sign an agreement that the owner will return the dog to the seller, and no one else, should the arrangement not work out.

Some adult Corgis may never have been exposed to or interacted with small children. If there are young children in your home, the first sight of these "miniature people" can be very perplexing to the inexperienced Corgi. When children run and play, the herding and heeling instinct in the Corgi may be aroused, perhaps leading to nipping at the children's feet and ankles. It may take considerable time and patience to overcome this inborn instinct but with perseverance and good judgment, most Corgis can be retrained.

A Training Regimen

Corgis were bred originally to work, and in order for them to learn to do their job they had to inherit a capacity and willingness to be trained. While this is obviously a great asset when properly directed, this capacity left untapped can result in a troublesome, some-times neurotic dog.

There are occasions upon which a breeder may be willing to place an entirely mature Corgi in a one-family home rather than having the dog spend the rest of its life as a kennel dog.

"Preschools" are an excellent way for young puppies to learn their early lessons and to become accustomed to strange dogs and people.

arrival. A good part of your puppy's safety depends upon your ability to properly "puppy-proof" your home.

◆ Electrical outlets, lamp cords, strings, and mouth-size objects of any kind all spell danger to the inquisitive puppy. If you think of your new arrival as both super sleuth and demolition expert, you will be better equipped to protect your puppy.

◆ All puppies are experts at getting into places they shouldn't be and the Corgi is certainly no exception. The important thing to remember is that your Corgi puppy will not be able to chew a hole in your rug or pull the tablecloth and all its contents down on top of itself if it can't get to these "no-no" items in the first place.

◆ Such things as household cleaning products, gardening supplies, and poisonous plants must be kept in securely latched cupboards or well above the Corgi puppy's reach.

◆ There are many houseplants that can make your puppy ill or even cause its death. Most veterinarians will be able to supply you with a list of plants that are poisonous to dogs.

Bitter Apple

There is a product called Bitter Apple that tastes just like it sounds—*terrible!* Bitter Apple is actually a furniture cream that is nonpoisonous and can be used to coat electrical wires and chair legs. In most cases dogs loathe its taste, but do note that we say "in most cases"

Prospective Corgi owners would wisely be committed to establishing and regularly following a training regimen with the dog they buy. Anyone who is not willing to invest the time and effort to provide his or her Corgi with the training it needs should really look to another breed. It makes no more sense to own a dog with a great capacity to learn and have it lie idly about than it would to own a high-spirited race horse that will be used only to take Sunday riders on leisurely walks through the park.

There is no question as to the trainability and intelligence of the Corgi. The only question that remains is the prospective owner's willingness and ability to provide the proper training and environment.

Puppy-proofing Your Home

When you've chosen your dog or puppy and have made arrangements to pick it up and bring it home, take the time to make your house or apartment a welcoming, safe haven for the new because there is always the occasional dog that is not in the least deterred by the unpleasant taste. For the average dog that the product does discourage, the cream can be used not only to protect household items but many breeders use the product on dogs to prevent them from chewing on themselves as well.

Plastic Tubing

For the dog that Bitter Apple does not keep from chewing, there is plastic tubing available at hardware stores that can be put around electrical cords and some furniture legs. Still, a bored and restless Corgi puppy can chew through plastic tubing quicker than most of us are capable of putting it down. The message here is to never underestimate the ability of your puppy to get into mischief! Make sure you have secured the household to avoid having the puppy do what it should not do in the first place.

Holiday Precautions

Without a doubt, the holidays can provide more possibilities for your puppy to find its way into trouble than any other time of year. All the precautions you must take during the normal course of the year still apply, but those special days (or weeks) of the year require even more diligence.

Strangers in the house: Most households experience more traffic flow during the holidays than they do at any other time of year. Guests unaccustomed to puppy ownership do not realize that leaving doors ajar can lead to disaster. Neither would they stop to think a little turkey bone could cause death or that unfamiliar food could cause acute diarrhea in a puppy. Mom is usually called upon to add

significantly to her normal duties during the holidays, so watching the puppy and keeping an eye on the guests should definitely be a family responsibility.

It is also worth remembering that everyone entering the household will adore your little rascal as much as you do. Puppies are not terribly discerning about who they give a big wet kiss to or on whose new dark suit they deposit their puppy hair. Be considerate of your guests and your Corgi by making sure guests *want* your fluffy bundle of hair and licks all over them.

Deck the halls: Those shiny decorations used at Christmas or paper ornaments and balloons for other holidays can continue to deck the halls, but make sure they do so well above puppy level!

Food treats: New puppy owners and guests often feel a need to share holiday treats with little Winston. Not only can unaccustomed food create an upset stomach, diarrhea is almost inevitably the result. Few households need a puppy with diarrhea, acute or otherwise, especially during holiday events.

Holidays are chocolate lovers' field days. Boxes of chocolate on low tables are an invitation to disaster to a puppy or even a mature dog. *Chocolate contains a natural caffeine called theobromine that has been known to kill some dogs!* Do not allow your Corgi to have chocolate, and caution family and friends never to allow it either.

Other Deterrents

There are baby gates to keep your puppy out and cages, kennels, and paneled fence partitions of various kinds to keep your puppy in. All this and a daily "Puppy-proofing Patrol" will help you and your pet avoid serious damage.

CARE OF YOUR PUPPY

Preparing for the New Puppy

Advance planning will help a great deal in easing the puppy's transition from its familiar surroundings to the new and strange world you are providing. If possible, visit your puppy several times while it is still in its original home so that you are not entirely a stranger.

Just as humans prepare for the arrival of their new baby by creating a checklist of things to do and equipment to buy, so should new Corgi owners be organizing their home for the arrival of the new puppy. A fenced-off area in the kitchen is the ideal place to start your puppy off; accidents can be easily cleaned up and the kitchen is a room in which there is normally a good deal of traffic and noise that can help accustom the youngster to day-to-day living.

Don't forget that a young puppy is accustomed to the companionship of its littermates. Without them the puppy will be lonely and it will be up to you to compensate for the loss of your puppy's siblings.

At the same time you must not let the puppy do whatever it chooses for the first few days and then suddenly expect it to start following rules that prohibit it from doing exactly

The young puppy needs to know it is secure and safe in its new home.

those same things. Being permissive in this respect is not being kind; it only serves to confuse the puppy.

Equipment and Toys

The following is a list of the basic requirements you should attend to well ahead of the day when your puppy is scheduled to arrive. The value and use of each will be more fully explained as we proceed.

Partitioned-off Living Area

Paneled fence partitions about 3 feet (91.5 cm) high are available at most major pet shops and are well worth the investment for keeping the puppy where you want it to be. These partitions can and will be useful in many ways for the rest of your dog's life. Corgi puppies love to be where their owners are but their constantly being underfoot can be hazardous to both puppy and owner. The safe area you create for the puppy will benefit you both.

Cage or Shipping Kennel

Inside the fenced-off area there should be a wire cage or fiberglass shipping kennel with a soft blanket or towel on the bottom for the puppy to snuggle into. This will very quickly become not only the puppy's "den" but also one of the best known methods of assisting

Corgi puppies and adults enjoy having toys to play with, but they should never be given items that have buttons or strings that can be chewed off and swallowed.

the two of you along the road to house-training (see page 59). These wire cages and fiberglass shipping kennels come in varying sizes. The number 300 size, which is approximately 32 inches (81 cm) long by 22 inches (56 cm) wide by 23 inches (58 cm) high will be the ideal size to accommodate the average Corgi through adulthood.

Water Dish and Feeding Bowl

These are available in many different materials. Choose something nonbreakable and not easy to tip over. A rambunctious Corgi puppy will very quickly learn to upset the water bowl and relish turning its entire living area into a swimming pool! Stainless steel bowls are recommended, as they eliminate the worry of

toxic content of some plastics, and Corgi puppies are not beyond chewing (and trying to digest) plastic bowls.

Breeder's Diet Sheet

It is highly unlikely that the puppy's breeder would not have furnished you with this information but should this be the case, there are many highly nutritious commercial brands of dog food available at pet stores. These foods come complete with feeding instructions but if you do not feel confident that you will make the right choice of food, veterinarians are always helpful in this area as well.

Brush and Comb

A young Corgi's coat does not require a great deal of grooming, but learning to be groomed is a very important lesson for the puppy to learn and the process should begin early. The equipment that you will need is described in detail in Bathing, Grooming, and Home Health Care, beginning on page 79.

Soft Collar and a Leash

There are soft fabric collars that weigh next to nothing that can be purchased at any pet shop. When you go to visit your puppy at the home or kennel that it will be coming from, take along a piece of string with which to measure the circumference of its neck. Then take this with you to the pet shop where you purchase your initial supplies and the owner will be able to assist you in obtaining the correct size collar for those beginning lessons. Lightweight plastic or fabric leashes are good for the young puppy as they will not weigh heavily on the puppy's neck.

Toys

Puppies need a lot of toys of different kinds to keep them occupied, exercised, and out of mischief. These can be anything you choose, but be sure they are safe, without buttons or strings that can be chewed off or swallowed.

◆ Avoid balls made of soft material that can be chewed apart. The Corgi has great strength in its jaws, even as a puppy, and can easily demolish things other dogs of its size cannot.

◆ Avoid hard plastic toys that can splinter.

◆ Make sure all toys are too large for the puppy to get into its mouth. Small toys can become lodged in the mouth and caught in the throat.

◆ Never give your Corgi puppy old and discarded shoes or stockings to play with. A puppy is unable to determine the difference between "old" and "new" and unless carefully watched may think it is perfectly all right to add your new Gucci loafers to its toy collection.

◆ A Kong toy is wonderful for a Corgi puppy as are most heavy rope toys. The Kong toy is especially good because it is made of nearly indestructible rubber. The toy has a hole in the bottom that a little dab of peanut butter or some other treat can be stuffed into and it will keep the puppy licking and chewing away for hours on end.

Bringing Your Puppy Home

The safest way to transport the puppy from the kennel to your home is to obtain a pet carrier or cardboard box large enough for the puppy to stretch out comfortably with sides that are high enough so that it cannot climb out. Put a layer of newspapers at the bottom

Don't forget that a young puppy is accustomed to the companionship of its littermates. Without them the puppy will be lonely. It will be up to its new owner to compensate for the loss of the puppy's siblings.

in case of accidents and a soft blanket or towel on top of that. Ideally, another family member or friend should accompany you to do the driving or hold the carrier that the puppy is in.

Helpful hint: When your puppy arrives at its new home it will be confused and undoubtedly whine in search of its littermates, especially at night when its littermates are not there to snuggle up to. For the first few nights after the new puppy arrives, we put a box next to the bed and let the newcomer sleep there. Should the puppy wake up crying in loneliness, a reassuring hand can be dropped down into the box and we have thus avoided having to trudge to a different part of the house to quiet the lonely puppy.

Letting the puppy "howl it out" can be a nerve-racking experience that could easily cost you, your family, and your neighbors nights of sleep. You might be amazed at just how loud

Children should never encourage a Corgi puppy's playful growling or "puppy bites." These are habits that are hard to break when the puppy matures.

and how persistent your puppy can be when it comes time to announce to the world that it is homesick and lonely.

The box-by-the bed method teaches the puppy two important lessons: first, that it is really not alone in the world and second, it helps the puppy transfer its dependency upon littermates and mother to you. Should you wish to transfer the puppy's sleeping quarters to a different part of the house later, you can do this more easily once the puppy has learned to be by itself for increasing periods of time.

Socialization and Safety

It is very important that you accustom the Corgi puppy to everyday events as soon as it is practical. Strange noises, children, and other animals can be very frightening when the puppy first encounters them.

Good breeders make it a point to expose their puppies to as many everyday sights and sounds as possible, but this is not always practical when there are many dogs to be taken care of. Therefore, it is up to you to gently and gradually introduce your puppy to such sounds as the garbage disposal, the vacuum cleaner, and the television set.

Ideally, the first time your puppy is exposed to a strange, loud sound you will be able to keep the sound limited to just a few seconds. Once the puppy learns that the sound does not present danger, you will be able to increase the length of time. Eventually, the puppy will take even the loudest sounds completely in stride.

Young Children

Regardless of whether the Corgi puppy has had prior experience with young children, the children themselves must be educated about what they may and may not do with the new puppy.

◆ Do not leave young children unsupervised with the puppy.

◆ Learning the gentle approach and exercising caution when the puppy is underfoot are things all children should know.

◆ Children should not encourage a Corgi puppy's playful "puppy bites" or having the puppy chase them around the yard in fun. Although growling, puppy biting, and chasing may appear cute and are harmless in the Corgi youngster, they are habits that can become extremely difficult to correct as the puppy matures.

◆ Never allow children to chase the puppy and do provide a place of refuge for the puppy when toddlers are about.

◆ Make sure children never touch the puppy when it is eating or when it has a bone or chew toy in its mouth.

Carrying Your Puppy

Learning to pick up and carry a Corgi of any age is very important. The Corgi's long back can be injured very easily by lifting the dog improperly. This is important for both children and adults to understand. Never pick up a Corgi by its front legs or by the scruff of its neck. This applies just as much to the young puppy as it does to the fully mature adult. Lifting any dog in this manner can cause injury and a Corgi is particularly vulnerable.

A Corgi puppy should be picked up with one hand under its chest and the other hand firmly supporting its hindquarters. This not only gives the puppy a feeling of security; it enables you to keep full control.

The adult dog should be picked up in the same manner but do remember the only thing small about a Corgi is its legs—the Corgi lifts much heavier than it looks! Be sure that you learn to lift heavy objects properly before attempting to pick up an adult Corgi. The proper way for a person to lift any heavy object is to bend his or her knees and squat down first. Do not bend over from the waist and reach down for any heavy object you wish to pick up, including your Corgi.

Warning: Only children old enough to safely hold and control a puppy should be allowed to pick it up at all. Corgi puppies are very active and quite strong for their size. They can suddenly squirm and jump out of a child's arms.

Learning how to pick up Corgis properly is important to avoid injuring their long backs. One hand should be placed under the chest; the other hand firmly supports the hindquarters.

A fall from any height can seriously and permanently injure a puppy.

Introducing Other Pets

The Corgi puppy's introduction to other animals in the household must also be carefully supervised. The average Corgi puppy loves the world and all creatures in it; however, even at a very early age Corgi puppies are inclined to be both a little bossy and incredibly inquisitive, two characteristics that can get a puppy into trouble with senior animals in the household.

The family cat that is not accustomed to dogs may react violently to the unwelcomed advances of the bold Corgi puppy. The adult dog with seniority may consider the new youngster an intrusion and mistake its exuberance for aggression. Little rodents or birds may represent toys to the Corgi, and naturally in a puppy's mind all toys belong in their mouths.

For all these reasons it is very important to confine the newcomer so that the other pets in the household are not constantly harassed

Corgis can be taught to get along well with all the family's other pets, but make sure introductions take place gradually and that each pet has an opportunity to get out of the way when it wishes to do so.

before they have had time to fully accept the puppy. The partitioned area set up to accommodate the new puppy that we described earlier will give the senior members of the household's animal kingdom an opportunity to inspect the new arrival at their leisure without having to endure unsolicited attention.

Once properly introduced and supervised, the Corgi and senior resident animals may or may not decide to become bosom buddies. Many Corgi owners tell of their dogs getting along

famously with resident dogs, cats, even other small animals—some to the point of appointing themselves guardians and protectors.

Car Travel

A part of a Corgi puppy's socialization process will take place away from home. The puppy must learn to accept strange people and places, and the only way for the puppy to learn to take these changes in stride is to visit as many new sites and meet as many strangers as you can arrange. Trips to the shopping mall or walks through the park will expose your young Corgi to new and different situations each time you are out. Of course this should never be attempted until your puppy has had all of its inoculations. Once that is completed, you are

both ready to set off to meet the world and this often involves riding in a car.

Most adult Corgis consider riding in the family car a highly anticipated treat. The moment most Corgis hear those car keys jingle, they are ready and willing to go. Puppies, however, can suffer varying degrees of motion sickness. The best way to overcome this problem, should it exist, is to begin with very short rides, such as once around the block. Ending the ride with a fun romp or a little food treat helps make the ride something to be enjoyed. The puppy should not be fed a full meal before the ride.

When the puppy seems to accept these short rides happily, the length of time in the car can be increased gradually until you see that the puppy is truly enjoying the outings. Even those dogs and puppies suffering the most severe cases of car-

As much as it might seem enjoyable to have your Corgi puppy or adult ride loose in the car, this can be extremely dangerous for both dog and driver. Both of you are much safer with the dog in its shipping kennel.

sickness seem to respond to this approach and soon begin to consider the car a second home.

Should your dog's carsickness continue, speak to your veterinarian. He or she can prescribe medication that can help to alleviate the problem.

Once your Corgi leaves your home it should be wearing its collar with identification tags attached. Many times, dogs are thrown clear of the car in an accident but become so frightened they run blindly away.

HOW–TO: HOUSE–TRAINING

The crate used for house-training should not be too large or the puppy will sleep at one end and eliminate in the other. It should be large enough to allow the puppy to stretch out comfortably, stand up, and turn around easily. Naturally, this creates a problem as the proper size crate for an eight-week-old puppy will not be the proper size for a six-month-old puppy. The easiest way to solve this is to use a piece of plywood to block off a part of the crate, adjusting the space accordingly as the puppy grows.

Your puppy's first experience with the crate will undoubtedly not be to the puppy's liking. Be prepared for some crying or whining. Some puppies will howl pitifully, sounding as if they are truly alone and abandoned forever.

Do not succumb to the puppy's laments; this is just what it is hoping to accomplish. Simply give the puppy a treat and if it begins to whimper use the *no* command that the two of you have been practicing right along since the first day you brought the youngster home.

Being Consistent

Young puppies will void both bowel and bladder almost immediately after eating, after strenuous play, and upon waking from a night's sleep or even a nap. Being aware of this will save many accidents. If, after each of these activities, you consistently take the puppy to the place designated for eliminating, you will reinforce the habit of going there for that purpose.

Only after seeing that Dutchess has relieved herself in both ways should you allow her to play unconfined and then only while you are there to watch what is happening. Should she begin to sniff the floor and circle around or squat down to relieve herself, say *"Dutchess, no!,"* pick her up immediately, and take her to the designated place. You will have to keep a watchful eye on the Corgi puppy with her little short legs. Corgi babies are so low to the ground that it is often hard to tell they are squatting until a little stream begins to emerge from under them!

When you are not able to watch what the puppy is doing indoors, she should be in the crate with the door latched. Each time you take the puppy to her crate, throw a small food treat into the crate and praise her as she enters the crate to go after the treat. If the puppy starts whining, barking, or scratching at the door because she wants to be let out, it is crucial that you do not submit to those demands. The puppy must learn not only to stay in her crate, but also to do so without complaining unnecessarily.

Every time the puppy begins to whine or bark, say *"No!"* very firmly. If necessary, give

Feeding in the Crate

Begin using the crate by feeding the puppy in it. Close and latch the door while she is eating. As soon as the food has been consumed, unlatch the crate door and *carry* her outdoors to the place where you want her to eliminate. Should you not have access to the outdoors, or feel you will later not be able to provide outdoor access for the house-trained dog, place newspapers or some other absorbent material in an out-of-the-way place that will remain easily accessible to the dog. Do *not* let the puppy run around or play after eating until you have carried her to the designated area. It is extremely difficult to teach a puppy not to eliminate indoors once she has begun to do so; therefore, it is very important to prevent accidents rather than correct them.

the crate a sharp rap with a rolled-up newspaper. It may take a good bit of persistence on your part, but patience will win out in the end.

Developing a Schedule

It is important to realize that a puppy of eight to twelve weeks will have to relieve its bladder every few hours except at night; therefore, you must adjust your schedule and the puppy's accordingly. You must also be sure Kipper has entirely relieved himself at night just before you retire and be prepared to attend to this the very first thing in the morning when you awake. How early in the morning Kipper needs his first outing will undoubtedly be determined by the puppy himself, but do not expect the young puppy to wait very long for you to respond to his "I have to go out now" signals. You will quickly learn to identify the difference between a puppy's signals that nature is calling and those that indicate he simply does not want to be confined.

Care and persistence in this project pays off very quickly with practically all Corgi puppies, and eventually you will begin to detect a somewhat anxious look or attitude in the puppy that indicates that he needs to relieve himself. Even the slightest indication in this direction should be met with immediate action on your part and accompanied with high praise and positive reinforcement.

When the Owner Is Away

The crate method of house-training is without a doubt the simplest and quickest method we have ever found to house-train a puppy. It is obvious, however, that this method cannot be used if you must be away from home all day or even for many hours at a time.

Again, we must stress that young puppies cannot contain themselves for long periods of

Crates used for house-training the young Corgi puppy should be just large enough to enable the puppy to stretch out comfortably. A piece of plywood can be used to block off excess space.

time. If the puppy must regularly be left alone for more than two or three hours at most, an alternative method must be used, but confinement is still the operative word for success.

For obvious safety reasons, a Corgi puppy should never be left to roam the house while the owners are away. It is dangerous for the puppy and accidents are bound to happen. The fenced-off area in the kitchen recommended for the arrival of the new puppy is the ideal place of confinement for your puppy while you are gone. The space should be only large enough to permit Kipper to eliminate away from the place in which he sleeps. The entire kitchen area is normally too large a space and creates the eliminating-at-random habit that is to be avoided at all cost.

The floor of the fenced-off area should be lined with newspaper. Kipper will become accustomed to relieving himself on the newspaper and this should become the "designated spot" to which you will take him when you are home and the puppy indicates he needs to eliminate. When you are home, you must insist the puppy use the newspapers every time.

BASIC PUPPY TRAINING

When to Begin

There was once a time when dog trainers and animal behaviorists believed that young puppies were entirely incapable of absorbing much in the way of learning until they were at least six months or older. Research and controlled experiments have now proven otherwise. In fact, puppy "preschools" are becoming increasingly popular throughout the country and to the benefit of the puppies themselves. Research has proven that puppies bred from stock of stable temperament have a tremendous capacity to learn, particularly during the critical socialization period of three to fourteen weeks.

Dr. Ian Dunbar, noted canine behaviorist, encourages early training and emphasizes that new owners who allow puppies to do anything they choose even in their first few days in their new homes are setting up a pattern for misbehavior. *Gentle*, *firm*, and *brief* seem to be the operative words in training young dogs and puppies; it can begin on the first day of the puppy's arrival.

Early Training

A young puppy's attention span is very short and puppies are incapable of understanding or retaining complex commands. This does not mean you should not begin simple basic training as soon as you bring your puppy home. It is much harder on the puppy to be chastised suddenly for something it has been allowed to do right along.

Although they are determined fellows, Corgis are also very sensitive to correction. A stern scolding will normally get your point across. *It is never necessary to strike a Corgi* (or any dog!). Your doing so may well have exactly the opposite of the effect intended. There are occasions when you may have to take sterner measures than a scolding but they can normally be accomplished by grabbing your dog by the ruff on both sides of the neck just behind the head and giving the dog a very firm and sharp *"No!"*

The Meaning of "No!"

One of the the most important commands your Corgi will ever learn is the word *"No!"* Just as important is your using the word only when you are prepared to enforce it. This is the only way the puppy will understand the true meaning of the word and, once understood, it can and will save both you and the puppy a great deal of unnecessary trauma.

The herding instinct of Welsh Corgis is very strong. Some of their instinctual behaviors are to be encouraged; others must be suppressed. The very first time your Corgi puppy nips at someone's heels (including your own) or growls when you attempt to take away a toy or bone, you must correct the puppy with a very firm *"No!"* Do not allow behavior of this kind to become established. As with all unwanted behavior in dog training, avoidance is more than half the battle.

"Come"

The next most important lesson for the puppy to learn is to come when called. This can be a somewhat bothersome lesson for the independent Corgi to learn but learning to come immediately when called could well save your dog's life when the two of you venture out into the world.

The first step is for the puppy to become familiar with his name. Right from the beginning include the puppy's name every time you speak to him: *"No, Winston, no!" "Good boy, Winston, good boy."* Every time you feed your puppy or give it a treat, use the puppy's name.

The *come* command is one a dog must understand has to be obeyed always and instantly, but the dog should not associate that command with fear. The dog's responding to his name and the word *"Come"* should always be associated with a pleasant experience such as great praise and petting or a food treat.

In dog training of any kind it is much easier to avoid the establishment of bad habits than it is to correct entrenched, undesirable behavior. Never give the *come* command unless you are sure your puppy will come to you. Initially, use the command when the puppy is already on his way to you or give the command while walking away from the youngster.

Very young puppies will normally want to stay as close to their owner as possible, especially in strange surroundings. When your puppy sees you moving away, his natural inclination will be to get close to you. This is a perfect time to use the *come* command.

Later, as the puppy grows more independent and perhaps a bit headstrong, you may want to attach a long leash or small rope to his collar to insure the correct response. Chasing or punishing your puppy for not obeying the *come* command in the initial training stages makes the youngster associate the command with something negative and will result in avoidance rather than the immediate positive response you desire. It is imperative that you praise your puppy when he does come to you, even if he delays responding for many minutes.

The Corgi trained to heel at its owner's side will make daily walks pleasurable.

Leash Training

It is never too early to accustom the puppy to a collar and leash; it is your way of keeping your dog under control. It may not be necessary for the puppy or adult dog to wear a collar and identification tags within the confines of your home and property, but no dog should ever leave home without a collar and without the leash held securely in your hand.

Begin getting your puppy accustomed to the collar by leaving it on for a few minutes at a time. Gradually extend the time you leave the collar on. Most puppies become accustomed to their collars very quickly and forget they are even wearing them.

Once this is accomplished, attach a light-weight leash to the collar while you are playing with the puppy in the house or in your yard. Do not try to guide the puppy at first. The point here is to accustom the puppy to the feeling of having something attached to the collar.

Encourage the puppy to follow you as you move away. Should he be reluctant to cooperate, coax him along with a treat of some kind. Hold the treat in front of the puppy's nose to encourage him to follow you. As soon as the puppy takes a few steps toward you, praise him enthusiastically and continue to do so as you move along.

Make the initial session very brief and very enjoyable. Continue the lessons in your home or yard until the puppy is completely unconcerned about the fact that it is on a leash. With a treat in one hand and the leash in the other you can begin to use both to guide the puppy in the direction you wish to go.

Once the collar and leash are accepted you can begin your walks near to the house and eventually around the block. You and your Corgi puppy are on your way to a lifetime of adventure together.

Crate Training

A wire cage and fiberglass shipping kennel, commonly known as crates, are invaluable in house-training your dog.

Some new dog owners who have purchased puppies from us have initially looked upon the crate method of confinement during house-training as cruel. More often than not, these same people have come back to thank us for suggesting the crate method as one of the most valuable training tips they have ever learned.

Using a properly sized crate reduces the average house-training time to a minimum and eliminates keeping the puppy under constant stress by correcting it for making mistakes in the home. Most dogs, and Corgis in particular, continue to use their crates voluntarily as a place to sleep, as it provides a sense of safety and security. It becomes their cave or den and in many cases a place to store their favorite toys or bones.

Those of us who live in an earthquake-prone area find our dogs will make a hasty retreat to their crates at the earliest sign of a tremor. Often we have found it necessary to become very persistent in order to get some dogs to emerge from their crates even after the quake has long passed.

Confining your dog is the only possible way to avoid having soiling accidents in the house. Corgis are instinctively clean animals and will not soil their immediate surroundings unless they have no choice.

CORGI CARE

Your Corgi

The Corgi's genetic makeup urges it to be continually active both mentally and physically. If you as an owner accommodate this activity, you will have a dog that will at times amaze you with its intelligence and readiness to learn. If you do not work with your Corgi do not be surprised if behavioral problems develop. Some breeds do well living outdoors in a run with only minimal human contact. Other breeds are perfectly content to lounge on the sofa all day with nothing more to do than sleep and eat. Corgis do not fall into either of these categories, particularly when they are young.

Most owners are quick to agree that failure to provide a Corgi with something to do will definitely inspire it to become quite creative on its own. That creativity, unfortunately, might prove terribly costly to the negligent owner, and the Corgi's determined nature will not have that established behavior easily dissuaded

Helpful hint: Plan on giving your Corgi time to "work." That work can take the form of anything as simple as fetching the newspaper, allowing your dog to perform its obedience repertoire, playing flyball or frisbee, or perfecting its agility or herding exercises. These activities are described in greater detail in the chapter titled Sharing Your Life with a Corgi, beginning on page 95.

Some Corgis will take on the duties of serving as nanny for the family children. Others will spend a good part of the day rounding up pet ducks or chickens and making sure they remain within view. See what your Corgi has a natural tendency toward and develop that. Activities combined with daily walks, grooming sessions, and simply having your Corgi sit beside you while you watch television or read will satisfy your dog's need for activity and human contact.

Outdoor Manners

Aggressive Dogs

Corgis may not be inherently quarrelsome but neither will they tolerate aggression on the part of other dogs. A Corgi will not back down to a bully, no matter how large and imposing that bully might be. You must assume the responsibility of having your dog under control at all times, even though other people may not be relied upon to do so. A leash and a collar are an absolute *must* any time your Corgi is not in your home or within the confines of your fenced-in property.

Children Playing

Young children are high-energy individuals and there is no way nor any need to keep them

Your Corgi looks to you for loving care.

from running and being noisy when they are outdoors playing. This can easily awaken the herding instinct in an untrained or uncontrolled Corgi that could dash off after the children, attempting to herd them, even attempting to nip at their heels. This can be both frightening and traumatic to a young child; being chased can easily cause the child to scream or cry and run even faster. This in turn excites and stimulates a herding dog and, needless to say, creates a situation that could have been easily avoided if the dog had been kept on a leash.

Gutter Training

Never let Dylan relieve himself where people might walk or children are playing. Try to teach him to use the gutter to relieve himself. Even then, you should always carry a small plastic bag to remove droppings immediately and dispose of them in a trash receptacle. Many city governments impose heavy fines on dog owners who do not pick up after their dogs.

Behavior Problems

Most of the behavior problems owners experience with their Corgis are due to the fault of the owner rather than the dog. One must not forget that a Corgi is first and foremost a dog, and one of the basic needs of all dogs is to have a pack leader. A pack leader sets boundaries and in so doing gives the members of the pack a sense of security.

Boundary setting and enforcing those boundaries do not intimidate dogs or diminish their capacity to learn. Setting limits actually establishes a line of communication between you and your dog that works for both of you.

Chewing

Puppies will chew. It helps them through their teething stages, and it exercises and strengthens their jaws. Grown dogs chew things because they enjoy it. Chewing relieves stress and boredom. Your dog must learn early on what it can and cannot chew. Half the battle is in preventing dogs from chewing the wrong things. Don't give your dog the opportunity to do so.

A dog cannot tell the difference between your discarded old slipper and your newest pair of dress shoes; both smell exactly like you and are just as chewable. Don't expect your dog to understand that it is acceptable to chew on one and not the other. Never give your dog any of your personal items to chew on; you must assist the dog's learning that none of the smell-just-like-you items are playthings.

Make sure your Corgi is confined to its crate or dog-proof room with something it is allowed to chew when you are not there to supervise. Does this sound cruel? Think again. Which is more cruel—safely confining your dog when you are not there or flying into a rage because the dog entertained itself by eating a hole in the sofa while you were gone?

House-training Problems

House-training is based upon Corgis' natural dislike for eliminating where they eat and sleep. A Corgi is a particularly clean dog but supervision is important in having the dog understand human cleanliness rules. Dogs do not have to eliminate near their food or sleeping place when given freedom of the whole house. For more on house-training, see pages 54–55.

Jumping Up

Even people who like dogs do not particularly enjoy being jumped up on when they enter someone's home. Consistency is the only thing that works here. Do not let your dog jump up on your leg or on anyone else's—ever. A leg is a leg, and if it is acceptable to jump up on yours for a pat, then in the dog's mind all other legs are fair game as well.

When Drover runs joyfully to greet you and jumps up for a pat, give the command "*Off!*" and push his paws off your leg. As soon as the dog's paws hit the floor, praise him lavishly. Remember: Everyone in the family must do this or it will not work. When you and Drover are away from home, have him under control on his leash and repeat the command when he attempts to jump up on strangers.

Teaching a dog not to jump up can be a problem in that other dog lovers will encourage your dog to jump up, offering, "I don't mind, I love dogs," as their reason. It is important for you to correct your dog and politely explain to the person encouraging the behavior that this can frighten other people and you are trying to teach your dog not to do this.

Separation Anxiety

The Corgi is a social creature and some of them become more upset at being left alone than others. This is called "separation anxiety" by dog behaviorists. This anxiety can manifest itself in barking, whining, or attempting to destroy things. All dogs must learn that your absence is simply a matter of routine. Don't treat your departure or return like the climax of a romance novel. Dogs get caught up in your emotional responses. If the dog relates your coming and going with hugging, kissing, and all kinds of heightened emotion, anxiety sets in.

Should you submit to Molly's protestations and allow her to roam the house while you are gone, you may return to find unpleasant results. Your reaction then signals your displeasure and makes the dog realize you are displeased. Thus, your dog begins to associate your departure with something unpleasant. This in itself can create stress for the dog, and dogs, like humans, can react erratically under stress.

All this can be eliminated by making sure Molly is safe and secure in her crate, cage, or, weather permitting, outdoor run while you are gone. A word of caution here, however. If you do leave your Corgi in your yard or run while you are away from home, make sure all gates are securely locked. Easily opened gates are an invitation to inquisitive children or, worse yet, to thieves. Feeling secure is the first step in your Corgi's "home alone" training. This nips in the bud any chance of destructive behavior. Going in and out of the room while the dog is confined is the next stage. The dog is learning that you do come back and coming or leaving means little or nothing.

Stepping out of the dog's sight but remaining within earshot comes next. The minute the barking or howling begins, you must command "*No!*" Increase the time you are out of sight but not out of earshot. Eventually, your absence will go by unnoticed. This may take longer to accomplish with some dogs than it does with others, but persistence is the key. When being left alone is no longer a traumatic experience, you can experiment with leaving the dog loose in a room or in the house if you wish, but again, this should be done gradually.

Digging

All dogs like to dig. Corgis love it! They do it to relieve boredom and to find a nice cool spot

to lie in. They do it to seek and destroy the creatures they know (or think they know) are hiding under the ground. Correcting the digging problem is not always easy.

Again, supervision works best. If it is not possible to supervise your dog while it is outdoors, keep it inside until you can be there to watch what is going on. The minute your dog attempts to dig, let it know with that tried-and-true *no* command that this is not acceptable. Good luck on this one!

Some Corgi owners have dealt with the digging problem by providing their dogs with a place to do just that. A pit at the back of one's property or in the corner of the yard can be

The Corgi is a social creature and some become more upset at being left alone than others. This is called "separation anxiety." Your dog must be taught that your absence is simply a matter of routine.

allocated for its digging needs, and with patience and supervision dogs can be trained to understand that their pit is the only place digging is allowed. You can encourage your dog to dig in its own pit by burying some delectable treasures there. Once or twice assist the dog in finding what is buried there and give lavish praise when the objects are found.

Spaying and Neutering

All companion Corgis, whether male or female, should be sexually altered unless specifically purchased to breed or to show. Only a Corgi purchased from a breeder who has recommended that it be bred should be allowed to have offspring. You would be astounded by how many dogs and cats are put to sleep each year because they have no homes. The American Humane Society estimates at least 15 million healthy, friendly dogs and cats were euthanized in 1998 alone!

We trust that you, as a responsible dog owner, would never allow your Corgi to roam the streets, nor would you consider turning it over to the dog pound; yet there is no way you can guarantee that someone who might purchase a puppy from you will not be irresponsible and permit the dog to roam or wind up being euthanized at the pound.

Parents who wish to have their young children "experience the miracle of birth" can do so by renting videos of animals giving birth. Handling the experience this way saves adding to pet overpopulation.

There is constant lobbying throughout America to restrict the rights of all dog owners and dog breeders because of this pet overpopulation and the unending need to destroy unwanted animals. Thoughtful dog owners will leave the breeding process to experienced individuals who have the facilities to keep all resulting offspring on their premises until suitable and responsible homes can be found for them.

Altering your pet can also avoid some of the more distasteful aspects of dog ownership. As previously discussed, males that have not been altered have the natural instinct to lift their legs and urinate on objects to mark the territory in which they live. It can be extremely difficult to teach an unaltered male not to do this in your home. Males also have a greater tendency to roam if there is a female in heat in the area.

The female will have two estrus cycles each year that are accompanied by a bloody discharge. Unless the female is kept confined, there will be extensive soiling of the area in which she is allowed and, much more disastrous, she could become mismated and pregnant. Unspayed females also have a much higher risk of developing pyometra or mammary cancer later in life.

Toys

The rules governing the selection of toys for a Corgi puppy apply throughout the lifetime of your dog.

◆ Never give a Corgi a toy that is small enough to fit in the dog's mouth or that can be chewed apart into small pieces. Very strong rubber rings and rope toys designed for large dogs are usually suitable for the Corgi.

◆ Some Corgis treasure teddy bears and other stuffed animals and keep them nearly intact for many years; however, in most cases toys of this kind can be dangerous. More than one dog has expressed its displeasure at being left behind by completely dismantling a favorite teddy bear or stuffed doll. The danger here is that the material with which the toy has been stuffed can be ingested and cause severe illness or even death.

Bones

Animal bones of any kind are not a wise choice for a Corgi. Corgis are capable of splintering even large knucklebones. Further, any traces of meat on the bone provide a breeding

Do not permit your puppy ever to growl or snap if you take away a toy or pick up its food dish. If you allow this behavior in a puppy, the adult Corgi will challenge you at every turn.

ground for bacteria and if the bone remains outside it can attract vermin.

The artificial, nonsplintering bones available at a pet supply store can provide every bit as much chewing exercise and teeth cleaning as animal bones and provide none of the dangers of the latter. Just make sure the artificial chew bones you purchase are larger than the size your Corgi can fit into its mouth or swallow.

Instilling Good Behavior

Responsible owners will have begun training when their Corgi arrived in their home. Trying to undo bad habits is extremely difficult with any dog and particularly so with Corgis who love and adapt to routine very quickly. For instance, if Duke has been permitted to sleep on his owner's bed or climb up on furniture for many months, he simply cannot understand why, starting today, this is no longer allowed.

You may well have a good reason for making this change, but you will be hard-pressed to make your Corgi understand this reason. What will result instead is a constant war; Duke will do everything in his power to resume his comfortable habit, and you will lose patience with his attempts to do so. You need not worry about hurting your Corgi's feelings with a strong reprimand so long as you are not unfair, inconsistent, or violent.

Aggression on the part of your Corgi should not be tolerated; avoid allowing it ever to start. Do not permit your puppy ever to growl or snap if you take away a toy or pick up its food dish. If you allow this behavior when your dog is a youngster, you can rest assured you will wind up with a Corgi that will challenge you at every turn as an adult. A sharp rap with your fingers on the nose of the puppy that is testing its dominance by growling or biting will not have any ill effects upon its development. It will, however, go a long way in preventing a dangerous problem from ever getting under way.

Corgis cannot be bullied. They will simply not respond to that kind of treatment. Clear consistent rules are what the breed needs and thrives on.

Training Classes

For obedience work beyond the basics, it can be extremely beneficial for the Corgi owner to seek out local professional assistance. There are free-of-charge classes at Department of Parks and Recreation facilities, as well as very formal

A leash and collar are an absolute must anytime your Corgi is not in your home or within the confines of your fenced-in property.

and sometimes very expensive individual lessons with private trainers. There are some obedience schools that will take your dog and train it for you; however, we find in the case of Corgis that there is no substitute for the rapport that develops when dog and owner train together.

Training classes are especially good for Corgis because they give them an opportunity to learn to respond in the midst of strange dogs and strange people. The classes are also a wonderful socialization opportunity for the dogs.

Traveling with Your Dog

At first thought, having your Corgi accompany you on your summer vacation may sound like great fun for both of you, but think this out carefully. Further consideration could well alter your decision:

◆ Finding a place for your Corgi to stay when you stop along the way to eat or to sleep can present considerable difficulties. Unlike most European countries, restaurants in America do not permit dogs to accompany their owners inside the establishment, and because of irresponsible owners, many hotels and motels do not permit dogs.

◆ Leaving your dog alone in a parked automobile while you eat in a restaurant can be very dangerous. Weather conditions can change rapidly and temperatures in a closed car can soar within just a few minutes.

◆ Many of the hotels and motels that do allow

pets into the rooms charge an extra fee or security deposit. These establishments also assume that your dog is accustomed to being left alone in a strange place and will not disturb other guests by barking and howling while you are out of your room.

◆ Changing your dog's accustomed food and water can create a number of problems, including diarrhea, not something most people wish to cope with while traveling.

Have a Good Trip

It should be easy to see that taking your Corgi along with you on a trip will require a great deal of advance planning:

◆ An air-conditioned car can help considerably if your trip will be made through areas where daytime temperatures are high.

◆ Take the crate or cage with you that you have been using at home. This keeps your

When traveling with your dog, it is important to remember restaurants do not permit dogs to accompany their owners inside as they do in many European countries.

pet safe while traveling and provides a safe, secure, and familiar place for the dog if you are out of your hotel room.

◆ Stops along the way must be carefully planned. Realize that your selection of restaurants will have to be made with your pet's safety in mind. At any stop your car must not be left in the sun. Further, unless the weather is very cool, windows should be left open if your dog is in a cage or crate and *your car must be where you or a member of your party can see it at all times!*

◆ Many people who travel with their pets make an early morning stop at a grocery store or carry-out restaurant and purchase their own food for the day. Meal stops can then be made at some shady spot along the way. Should you decide to do this, it will also give you an opportunity to exercise your dog at the same time.

◆ Dinnertime for yourself should come after you have checked into your hotel or motel, fed and exercised your dog, and made sure the dog has settled down with blanket and toy.

◆ Reservations must be made in advance with those places that allow dogs in the rooms. If you have taken our previous advice and trained your Corgi to stay alone in its kennel or cage, you will not have to worry about barking and howling while you are gone, nor will you run the risk of having your dog cause any damage to the room.

◆ Some of the major hotel chains do accept dogs; others do not. The situation is easy to check out by calling any hotel chain's 800 telephone number and making inquiries about the specific hotel you plan on stopping at. It is best to make your reservation at that time and be sure to get a reservation confirmation number.

Leaving Your Dog Alone

If you have not accustomed your dog to being left alone in its kennel, it is to be hoped that it has at least learned to be left alone. If so, we seriously advise closing your Corgi in the bathroom while you are out of the hotel room. At any rate, it is very important to leave a "Do Not Disturb" sign on your door while you are gone to avoid a staff person's entering your room. An unsuspecting maid can open the door to your room and allow your dog to escape. Further, many Corgis consider guarding your temporary accommodations from intrusion just as important as guarding your regular home.

If your dog will not stay alone in a strange room without barking, *do not leave it alone!* The dog can become frenzied and destroy things or disturb the other occupants of the hotel. This happens time after time and creates a bad name for dogs and dog owners. You must be considerate of others, both people who are not particularly dog-tolerant as well as those who might wish to stay at the same hotel later with their own dog. The management of the hotel will not be disposed to allow other people with dogs to stay if you have abused your privileges.

Food and water: You must take along an adequate supply of your Corgi's accustomed food and water. Changing diets and water can seriously upset your dog, and diarrhea and vomiting are the last things you will want to deal with in your hotel room or on the road.

Grooming equipment: Do take along grooming necessities including your dog's brush and comb and a good flea and tick spray. If you plan to hike or walk your dog along the side of the road, these accessories will enable you to get rid of any unwanted debris or parasites your Corgi's coat might have attracted.

Travel Alternatives

Many dog owners are surprised to find their dogs actually *enjoy* their stay in a boarding kennel. Towser would undoubtedly enjoy a week or two in a boarding kennel that allows him to run, play, and bark at the other dogs all day in an outdoor fenced enclosure far more than being confined to a hotel room or car.

There are many excellent boarding kennels located around most towns and cities that offer facilities that will satisfy the needs of both you and your dog. Speak to your veterinarian or friends who are familiar with the boarding operation before leaving your dog, and personally inspect the facility yourself.

Should you be convinced that Towser could never be happy in a boarding kennel, there are responsible, bonded, and experienced pet sitters who will come to your home and stay with your pet while you are away. Your veterinarian may be able to supply you with the names of individuals who are experienced at providing this kind of service. It is always wise to ask for references from the individuals who provide this service and it is important that the references be checked out thoroughly.

Words of Caution on Dogs and Cars

As much as it might seem more enjoyable to have your Corgi puppy or adult ride loose in the car or on the seat beside you, this can be extremely dangerous. An overly enthusiastic canine passenger can interfere with the driver's control or divert the driver's attention. Also, a sudden stop can hurl your dog against the front window, severely injuring or even killing it.

The safest way to transport your Corgi is in a carrier with the door securely latched. Many station wagons accommodate partitions commonly referred to as "dog guards." These safety devices confine dogs to the rear portion of the car. These simple safety precautions might one day save the life of your pet.

Tags: Once your Corgi leaves your home it should be wearing its collar with identification tags attached. Many times, dogs are thrown clear of the car in an accident but become so frightened they run blindly away. Not knowing where they are and not carrying any means of identification, a dog may be lost forever.

Closed Windows: It is important to make it a practice never to leave your dog alone in the car with the windows closed. Even on cool

days the sun beating down on a closed car can send the inside temperature soaring. Leaving a Corgi alone in an unventilated car could easily cause its death.

The only time a dog should be left alone in a car is when conditions permit the windows to be left open. But this in itself is dangerous in that open windows risk escape and invite theft. Thieves are not beyond stealing dogs! A loose dog in a car with open windows courts disaster.

Requirements and Regulations

Bordering countries and even adjoining states can have specific rules and regulations regarding dogs and most other pets. For exam-

The well-bred Corgi can be both a champion in the show ring and a fine herding dog back on the farm.

ple, although Hawaii is part of the United States, you are not permitted to take your dog into that state—or any of the islands of the South Pacific for that matter—without leaving it in an official quarantine station for a length of time designated by the state government.

This also applies to several countries, including Great Britain, Australia, and some Scandinavian countries. You should never attempt to travel to any foreign country without first

checking with the consulate for that country regarding any requirements or regulations regarding pets.

Even in the United States, state laws vary regarding canine health requirements. Crossing the line into another state may necessitate that your dog have an inoculation not required where you live. Some states and cities have

Your well-behaved Corgi is welcome at many country inns and city hotels throughout the United States.

regulations demanding that certain breeds be kept muzzled at all times. Ignorance of the laws or regulations is seldom a valid excuse.

HOW-TO: COMMANDS

The Sit and Stay Commands

Equal in importance to the *no* command and learning to come when called are the *sit* and *stay* commands. Young puppies can learn the *sit* command quickly, especially if it appears to be a game and a food treat is involved.

First, it is important to remember that the Corgi-in-training must be on collar and leash for this and all other lessons. This will avoid the possibility of the dog dashing off to avoid doing something it might not want to do at that moment.

Sit: Give the *sit* command and immediately push down on Towser's hindquarters. Praise him lavishly when he does sit, even though it is you who made the action take place. A food treat always

Even young puppies can learn their basic obedience lessons. Here a young owner is teaching his puppy to sit on command.

seems to get the lesson across more quickly.

Continue holding Towser's rear end down, repeating the *sit* command several times. If he makes an attempt to get up, repeat the command while exerting pressure on the rear end until the correct position is maintained. Make your dog stay in this position for increasing lengths of time, beginning with a few seconds and increasing the time as lessons progress over the following weeks.

Stay: Once the *sit* lesson has been mastered, start on the *stay* command. With Towser on a leash and facing you, command him to sit. Take a step or two back and if he attempts to get up to follow you, say firmly, *"Sit-stay!"* At the same time, raise your hand, palm toward the dog, and again command *"Stay!"*

Any attempt on your dog's part to get up must be corrected immediately, returning him to the sit position and repeating *"Stay!"* Once your dog begins to understand what he must do, you can gradually increase the distance you step back from a few steps to several yards. Your Corgi eventually must learn that the *sit-stay* commands must be obeyed no matter how far away you are.

Later, with advanced training, your dog will learn that the command is obeyed even when you move completely out of sight.

Down: Once your dog has mastered the *sit* and *stay* commands, you may begin work on *down*. This is especially useful if you want your dog to remain in a particular place for a long period of time. *Down* is the one-word command for *lie down*. *Down* must only be used when you want the dog to lie down. If you want your dog to get down from the sofa or to stop jumping on you, use the *off* command.

Early in the training there can be a little more resistance to obeying the *down* command than there was to the *sit* command. Once a dog has become accustomed to lying down on command, it seems to be more relaxing for the dog and it seems less inclined to get up and wander.

Since Corgis are so low to the ground, you may have to begin this lesson on your knees with your dog sitting in front of and facing you. Give the command *"Dutchess, down!"* Then reach out and slide her front feet toward you. She will then automatically be lying down. Again, praise and a food treat are

You may have to assist the learning Corgi to assume the "down" command by sliding the puppy's front legs out ahead of it.

The Training Collar and Leash

We have found a lightweight, chain-link training collar to be very useful for all obedience training, particularly for the heeling lesson. It provides quick pressure around the neck and a snapping sound, both of which get the dog's attention. Erroneously referred to as a "choke collar," the chain-link collar used properly will not choke the dog.

Remember to remove the training collar when lessons are over. Because training collars have a loose fit, dogs can catch their paw on these collars or catch them on objects and injure or strangle themselves.

As soon as Winston has learned to walk along on the leash, insist that he walk on your left side. A quick short jerk on the leash will keep him from lunging from side to side, pulling ahead, or lagging behind.

appropriate. Continue assisting your Corgi into the *down* position until she does so on her own. Be firm and patient. Obeying this command can take a bit of time before some dogs respond, even when they understand fully what it is you want them to do.

Heel: Teaching your Corgi to heel is the very basis for off-leash control. In learning to heel, your dog will walk on your left side with its shoulder next to your leg no matter which direction you might go. We do not advocate ever having your dog off-leash when away from home, but it is reassuring to know that your dog will obey and stay with you regardless of circumstances. It should be easy to see how important a lesson this will be for safety's sake.

A lightweight, link-chain training collar is very useful for obedience training.

FEEDING YOUR CORGI

Your Corgi can be put on an adult feeding schedule at about ten months of age. This means it can be given one main meal a day, preferably at the same time each evening. Some owners prefer to divide the single meal into two smaller meals given morning and evening.

Meals can be supplemented by a morning or midday snack and for this we highly recommend hard dog biscuits made for large dogs.

There is no simple way to answer the question of what is the best food to give your Corgi. We have spoken to successful Corgi breeders in many parts of the world and each breeder we have spoken to seems to have their own tried-and-true method. Probably the best answer to the question is: Feed what works best, not necessarily what the dog likes best. Who can tell you just what food that is? We strongly recommend you consult with the breeder from whom you purchased your Corgi and with your veterinarian.

Amount to Feed

The correct amount of food to maintain a Corgi's optimum condition varies as much from dog to dog as it does from human to human. It

is impossible to state any specific *amount* of food your dog should be given. Much depends upon how much your dog exercises. A Corgi that spends the entire day working livestock will need considerably more food than the house dog whose exercise is limited to 20 or 30 minutes a day retrieving a ball.

Generally speaking, the amount of food for a normally active Corgi is the amount it will eat readily within about 15 minutes of being given the meal. What your dog does not eat in that amount of time should be taken up and discarded. Leaving food out for extended periods of time can lead to erratic and finicky eating habits.

It must be remembered that the Corgi was originally bred to be a working dog. Meals were sporadic, of questionable nutritional value, and came only after a long grueling day's work. Today's Corgi has an appetite every bit as big as that of its ancestors but usually has far less work to do. Corgis can gain weight very easily if their food intake is not controlled and they are not given an opportunity to get sufficient exercise.

A good rule of thumb to follow in determining whether or not a Corgi is receiving the proper amount of food is to closely monitor the dog's condition. You should be able to feel the ribs and backbone through a slight layer of muscle and fat.

This foxy-faced Corgi is content after a good dinner.

Essential Nutrients

Fresh water and a properly prepared balanced diet containing the essential nutrients in correct proportions are all a healthy dog needs to be offered. If your Corgi will not eat the food offered, it is because it is either not hungry or it is ill. If the former is the case, the dog will eat when it is hungry. If you suspect the latter, an appointment with your veterinarian is in order.

Dogs, whether Corgis or Great Danes, are carnivorous (meat-eating) animals, and while the vegetable content of your dog's diet should not be overlooked, a dog's physiology and anatomy are based upon carnivorous food acquisition. Protein and fat are absolutely essential in a dog's diet. The animal protein and fat your dog needs can be replaced by some vegetable proteins, but the amounts and the kind require a better understanding of nutrition than most people have.

There are so many excellent commercial dog foods available today that it seems a waste of time, effort, and money to try to duplicate the nutritional content of these well-thought-out products by cooking food from scratch. It is important though that you read labels carefully or consult with your veterinarian, who will assist you in selecting the best moist or dry food for your Corgi.

Canned Food or Dry?

A great deal of research is conducted by manufacturers of the leading brands of dog food to determine the exact ratio of vitamins and minerals necessary to maintain your dog's good health. Research teams have determined the ideal balance of minerals, protein, carbohy-

drates, and trace elements for a dog's well-being. Dog food manufacturing has become so sophisticated it is now possible to buy food for dogs living almost any lifestyle from sedentary to highly active. This applies to both canned and dry foods, but like most other things in life, you get what you pay for. It costs the manufacturer more to produce a nutritionally balanced, high-quality food that is easily digested by a dog than it does to produce a brand that provides only marginal nourishment.

By law, all dog food must list all the ingredients in descending order by weight. The major ingredient is listed first, the next most prominent follows, and so on down the line.

A diet based on meat or poultry (appearing first in the ingredients list) is going to provide more nutrition per pound of food than one that lists a filler grain product as the major ingredient. The diet based on meat and poultry will also cost more than a food heavy in inexpensive fillers.

Whether canned or dry, look for a food in which the main ingredient is derived from meat, poultry, or fish. Remember, you cannot purchase a top-quality dog food for the same price as one that lacks the nutritional value you are looking for. In many cases you will find your Corgi not only needs less of the better food, but there will be less fecal waste as well.

The Looks of Dog Food

The better dog foods are not normally manufactured to resemble products that appeal to humans. A dog does not care that a food looks like a sirloin steak or a wedge of cheese; all a dog cares about is how food smells and tastes. The "looks like" dog foods are manufactured to

An ever-increasing variety of food is on the market. Choose carefully so you can offer your Corgi the optimal mix of nutrients.

tempt the dog's owner, but since it is highly unlikely that you will be eating your dog's food, do not waste your money.

Be aware of canned or moist products that have the look of "rich red beef," or dry food that is red in color. In most cases, the color is put there to appeal to *you* and is achieved through the use of red dye. Dyes and chemical preservatives are no better for your dog than they are for you. A good red dye test is to place a small amount of canned or well-moistened dry food on a piece of white paper towel. Let the food sit there for about a half hour and then check to see if the towel has been stained. If the toweling has taken on a red stain, you can rest assured the color is there to appeal to your eye and not your dog's nutritional needs.

Special Diets

A good number of dog food manufacturers now produce special diets for overweight, underweight, and older dogs. While the amount of these foods may remain the same as standard products, the calorie content is adjusted to suit the particular problem that accompanies each of these conditions.

There is no better remedy for these conditions, however, than using good common sense. Obviously, too many calories and too little exercise will increase weight; fewer calories and an increase in physical activity reduces weight.

The geriatric or overweight dog needs a much lower-calorie diet than the growing puppy or adult dog of normal weight. It is also important to make sure your older dog gets its fair share of exercise each day. The elderly dog may prefer to spend more of its day on the sofa than when it was a youngster, but moderate exercise even for the very old dog will keep your friend alive longer.

BATHING, GROOMING, AND HOME HEALTH CARE

Equipment

Your Corgi will not require much of your time or equipment in the way of grooming but that is not to say that it needs no care at all in this respect. While the Corgi's coat may be referred to by some as "wash and wear," regular brushing keeps the coat clean, odor-free, and healthy. Most Corgis will shed their coats twice a year. Brushing is an absolute necessity at this time, particularly if your dog spends time indoors.

Regular grooming gives you the opportunity to keep on top of your dog's home health care needs. Such things as clipping nails, cleaning ears, and checking teeth can be taken care of during the time set aside for grooming.

Grooming Table

Investing in a grooming table that has a non-slip top and an arm and noose can make all of these activities infinitely easier. These tables are available at pet shops and it is important to choose a table with a height that allows you to stand or sit comfortably while you are working on your dog.

Do not attempt to groom or attend to your dog's health care while you and the dog are sitting on the floor. You will spend most of

Groom your Corgi with a firm and gentle hand, and it will enjoy the attention.

your time chasing the dog around the room and your Corgi will simply wander off when it feels it has had enough of your attention.

Brushes, Combs, Clippers

Invest in a good stiff bristle brush, a steel comb, and animal nail clippers or a nail grinder that grinds the nails down rather than actually cutting them. You will be using this equipment for many years so buy the best equipment you can afford.

The Corgi is a natural breed with a coat that requires no clipping or trimming. Proper brushing and a few snips of the scissors around the feet are all the grooming it will ever need.

Brushing

Undoubtedly, the breeder from whom you purchased your Corgi will have begun to accustom the puppy to grooming just as soon as there was enough hair to brush. You must continue on with grooming sessions or begin them at once if for some reason they have not been started. It is imperative you both learn to cooperate in this endeavor in order to make it an easy and pleasant experience.

Brush with the lay of the hair and use the steel comb on the longer hair of the "pants" on the dog's rear legs and, in the case of the Cardigan, on the tail. At shedding time there

Regular grooming sessions help keep an owner on top of a Corgi's home health care needs by staying ahead of any problems that might develop.

will be a tremendous amount of hair collected in your brush and comb. You can hasten this process by giving your Corgi a warm bath once the shedding has begun. This loosens the hair and, though you may think your dog will complete the process completely bald, fear not—

Necessary Grooming Equipment
◆ Grooming table
◆ Stiff bristle or wire brush
◆ Steel comb
◆ Nail clippers or nail grinder
◆ Scissors
◆ Rubber mat
◆ Spray hose
◆ Cotton balls
◆ Shampoo
◆ Washcloth
◆ Heavy towels

once the dead coat has been removed, the shedding stops and new hair growth will begin.

Foot Care

This is a good time to accustom your Corgi to having its nails trimmed and its feet inspected. Always inspect your dog's feet for cracked pads. Check between the toes for splinters and thorns, paying particular attention to any swollen or tender areas.

We suggest attending to your dog's nails every other week. The nails of a Corgi that spends most of its time indoors or on grass when outdoors can grow long very quickly. Do not allow the nails to become overgrown and then expect to cut them back easily. Each nail has a blood vessel running through the center called the *quick.* The quick grows close to the end of the nail and contains very sensitive nerve endings. If the nail is allowed to grow too long, it will be impossible to cut it back to a proper length without cutting into the quick. This causes severe pain to the dog and can also result in a great deal of bleeding that can be very difficult to stop.

Should the quick be nipped in the trimming process, there are any number of blood-clotting products available at pet shops that will almost immediately stem the flow of blood. It is wise to have one of these products on hand in case your dog breaks a nail in some way.

Bathing

Dog show exhibitors use coat care products that adhere to the Corgi's hair, and most exhibitors bathe their dogs before shows. Even at that, some exhibitors do use "dry bath" products rather than the tub and shampoo

Unless a Corgi is getting plenty of exercise on rough hard pavement or cement, the nails must be trimmed with canine nail clippers.

Another method of nail care is using a drumel, which grinds the nail instead of cutting it.

method. Well-kept Corgis are literally odor-free and frequent bathing is unnecessary.

When your Corgi does require a wet bath, you will need to gather the necessary equipment ahead of time:

◆ A rubber mat should be placed at the bottom of the tub to keep your dog from slipping and thereby becoming frightened.

◆ A rubber spray hose is absolutely necessary to thoroughly wet the coat. It is also necessary to remove all shampoo residue.

◆ A small cotton ball placed inside each ear will prevent water from running down into the dog's ear canal.

◆ Be very careful when washing around the eyes as soaps and shampoos can be extremely irritating.

◆ It is best to use a shampoo designed especially for dogs; the pH balance is adjusted to keep drying to a minimum and leaves the hair shining and lustrous.

Technique

In bathing, first soak the coat thoroughly with the spray hose. Then apply the shampoo

and start lathering behind the ears and work back. Use a washcloth to apply the soap and to rinse around the head and face. Once you have shampooed your dog, you must rinse the coat thoroughly, and when you feel quite certain all shampoo residue has been removed, rinse once

Each of a dog's nails has a blood vessel running through the center called the quick. The quick grows close to the end of the nail and contains very sensitive nerve endings. When clipping the nails it is important to avoid cutting into the quick.

Fresh water and a properly prepared balanced diet combined with sufficient exercise will keep your Corgi in optimum condition.

relieve the eye of debris and pollen. If your dog's eyes water continuously, have your veterinarian inspect them for a condition called entropion, in which the eyelid is inverted and the eyelashes cause irritation to the eye. It can be corrected by surgery. Entropion is rare in Corgis but has been reported in some instances.

Ear Cleaning

The insides of the ears should always be clean and pink. Nothing other than a cotton swab or ball should ever be inserted into the ear itself and never probe into the inner recess of the ear. Use the swab or cotton ball moistened with olive or almond oil to clean the ear. If wax has accumulated, dip the swab or cotton ball into rubbing alcohol, squeeze out the excess thoroughly, and clean out the ear.

Do not attempt to treat an ear that has an unpleasant odor. Consult your veterinarian immediately; the odor may indicate the presence of parasites in the ear, or worse, there may be an ear infection.

Anal Sacs

The anal sacs (also referred to incorrectly as the anal *glands*) are located on each side of the anus and should be regularly looked after. They can become blocked, causing extreme irritation and abscesses in advanced cases.

If you notice your Corgi pulling itself along the ground when it is sitting down, you should check the anal glands. While not a particularly pleasant part of keeping your dog healthy, if

more. Shampoo residue in the coat is sure to dry the hair and could cause skin irritation.

As soon as you have completed the bath, use heavy towels to remove as much of the excess water as possible. Your dog will undoubtedly assist you in the process by shaking a great deal of the water out of its coat on its own.

Home Health Care

It is important to establish a weekly health care routine for your Corgi. Maintaining this schedule will prevent escalation of serious problems that may require expensive veterinary attention.

Eye Care

If the eyes are inflamed or discharging any kind of matter, check for foreign bodies such as soot or weed seeds. Regular flushing of the eye with cotton and cool water will help

regularly attended to, keeping the anal glands clear is relatively easy.

The best time to attend to this job is when you are giving your dog its bath. With the dog in the tub, place your thumb and forefinger of one hand on either side of the anal passage and exert pressure. The glands will empty quickly. Wear rubber gloves when performing this function and it is best to cover the anus itself with cotton or tissue. Should you be unsure of how to perform this procedure, your veterinarian or the breeder from whom you purchased your Corgi will be able to instruct you or, better yet, do it for you!

Dental Care

Care should always be given to the state of your dog's teeth. If your dog has been accustomed to chewing hard dog biscuits or gnawing on large rawhide or artificial bones since puppyhood, it is unlikely that you will have any problems as this chewing activity assists greatly in removing dental plaque, which is the major cause of tooth decay. Any sign of redness of the gums or tooth decay requires expert attention.

Retention of baby teeth can cause long-term problems with the permanent teeth. Generally, by the time the permanent teeth have come through at about five months of age, the Corgi's baby teeth have all fallen out. If there are any baby teeth remaining at this stage, seek your veterinarian's advice on their removal; retaining baby teeth can interfere with the proper placement of your Corgi's permanent teeth.

Your Corgi can pick up ticks and fleas in grass, wooded areas, or even sand at the beach.

Parasites

Fleas

While fleas are a problem everywhere, these pests can be especially troublesome for those who live in climates that have no freezing temperatures to kill off the existing infestation. Granted, the flea force returns just as soon as the warmer weather sets in, but there is at least some respite. The more temperate climates do not even have this relief.

As fastidious as you might be about caring for your Corgi and keeping its coat in good condition, you must be aware that fleas will still be a problem. Even if you were to protect your Corgi as you would a hothouse flower, its daily walks can bring fleas into your home and once there, the little creatures multiply with alarming rapidity.

Dips, sprays, and bombs: Bathing or "dipping" your Corgi with a good flea soap or product manufactured to eliminate fleas is not

enough. If you find fleas—even one flea—on your dog, there are undoubtedly hundreds of others lurking in the carpeting and furniture, just waiting for your dog to emerge from the tub so that they can hop back on.

The only way to combat fleas is to rid dog, house, and yard of the problem all at the same time. Simultaneously with your dog's flea bath, you must eliminate fleas from within your home and surrounding outdoor premises.

Flea bombs manufactured for this purpose are available at most hardware stores and veterinary offices. If your Corgi, like most dogs, spends any time at all in your yard or garden, you must also spray that area with one of the many products available at pet shops and hardware stores.

The most efficient way to eliminate the flea problem is to arrange for your Corgi to have a flea bath at the local dog-grooming salon. Make an appointment to have a commercial pest control service come to your home while your dog is at the groomer. The service will spray both the interior of your home and the surrounding property as well. Most of these companies guarantee their work for a specific period of time and many offer a monthly or quarterly plan by which they will return to make sure the problem does not get out of hand again.

Flea collars: The latest advance in flea collars is one that emits an artificial hormone that inhibits the development of any larva that can be deposited on your dog by a live flea. This must be accompanied by a complete and repeated flea elimination program in the household and surrounding area.

Lack of success in the use of the bathing and collar methods described is more apt to be the result of not following product instructions.

There is also a good possibility of toxicity when using flea sprays or flea collars; therefore, it is very important to read instructions on the packaging of these items very carefully.

Flea pills and liquids: Pills have been developed that, administered orally once a month, condition the dog's system to completely interfere with the maturation of eggs and larval fleas. The pills also prevent the fleas from becoming normal, reproducing adults. After biting the dog, the flea passes on the inhibitor to its offspring.

The liquid applications operate in exactly the same way but are placed on the skin between the dog's shoulder blades where the dog is unable to reach with its tongue. The liquid is absorbed within a matter of hours.

The pills and liquids do not entirely eliminate mature fleas. Sprays and soaps must still be used to eliminate the existing adult fleas, but a combination of prescribed pill use and local applications of flea products can eventually eliminate the problem.

Lice

Lice are seldom a problem with the well-cared-for Corgi, because the pests are spread by direct contact. In other words, to have lice your dog must spend time with another animal that has lice or be groomed with a contaminated brush or comb. Since these pests are minute in size, they are not as easy to see as fleas.

If no fleas are present and you suspect lice, the dog must be bathed with an insecticidal shampoo every week until the problem is eliminated. Fortunately, unlike fleas, lice live and breed entirely on the dog, so it is not necessary to treat the entire area in which the dog lives.

Ear Mites

Ear mites are parasites that settle in the external ear canal and can lead to chronic irritation. Symptoms are an extremely disagreeable odor, a dark waxy secretion, and constant scratching at the ear by the dog. Once present, ear mites can be extremely persistent, particularly if a dog becomes severely infested. Flushing of the ear by a veterinarian is recommended.

Ticks

Ticks are bloodsucking insects that bury their heads firmly into the skin. Your Corgi can pick up ticks by running through grass, wooded areas, or even through sand at the beach. They can become a source of extreme irritation to your dog and can cause secondary infections as well. It is important to loosen the tick's grip before you attempt to remove it; otherwise, you may allow the head to break away from the tick and remain lodged in the dog's skin. This also can cause severe infections.

To remove adult ticks, soak them with a spray made especially for tick removal; once the parasite has loosened its grip, you can remove it with a pair of tweezers. Regular bathing with a tick dip will prevent reinfestation, but, as is the case with all dips and sprays, you must read the instructions carefully as some of these products may be toxic.

Many of the new flea-control pills and liquids also act against tick infestation. These are only available through your veterinarian, so consult him or her about which of the products may be best for your Corgi.

The entire environment in which the dog lives must be regularly and vigorously treated against ticks, especially if you live adjacent to a wooded area. Ticks can transmit serious diseases that can endanger humans as well as animals. In some areas ticks carry Lyme disease, babesiosis, erlichiosis, and Rocky Mountain spotted fever. It is important that you discuss the tick problem with your local veterinarian, who can advise you on which dangers might present themselves.

Vomiting and Diarrhea

Perhaps the most common canine ailments are vomiting and diarrhea. They do not indicate that your dog is seriously ill but, should either symptom persist for more than 24 hours, you should call your veterinarian. Young puppies should be seen sooner as they can quickly dehydrate.

Evidence of blood, either "coffee ground" in appearance in vomit or black and tarlike in stools, warrants an immediate visit to your veterinarian.

Dogs may vomit to purge their digestive tracts. Puppies may do so when they overeat or eat too much or too fast. Intense exercise directly after eating can cause vomiting. None of this is cause for alarm unless it occurs repeatedly.

For occasional diarrhea, change from your dog's regular diet to thoroughly cooked rice, to which a small amount of boiled chicken has been added. Maintain this diet until the condition improves and then gradually return your dog to its normal diet.

ACCIDENTS AND ILLNESSES

Minor accidents and illnesses will undoubtedly occur while your Corgi progresses through puppyhood, adolescence, and on into old age. This chapter is written in the hope that it will assist the owner of a pet Corgi to determine the difference between situations that can easily be taken care of at home and those that demand veterinary treatment.

There is one piece of advice that always applies: If you are in doubt about the seriousness of your dog's problem, do not hesitate to consult your veterinarian.

Immunizations

Very effective vaccines have been developed to combat diseases that once were fatal to practically any infected dog. The danger of a Corgi being infected with distempter, hepatitis, leptospirosis, or the extremely virulent parvovirus is highly unlikely if proper inoculations and booster shots have been given regularly. Rabies among well-cared-for dogs is practically unheard of, but dogs that come in contact with animals in nature can be at risk if not immunized. Your veterinarian may also recommend immunizations against kennel cough, Lyme disease, and coronavirus.

Immunization against these infectious diseases begins in puppyhood and it is extremely

Your sweet Corgi trusts you to take good care of her and act quickly if anything goes wrong.

important that you follow your veterinarian's inoculation schedule; neglecting to do so could easily cost your dog's life. On occasion, however, there are dogs that, for one reason or another, do not develop full immunity. Any marked change in your dog's behavior should be observed very closely, especially if your dog is under one year.

Should your dog suddenly become listless, refuse food, and start to cough and sneeze, contact your veterinarian at once. Other signs of possible problems in this area are marked increase in thirst, blood in the stools or urine, and discharge of any kind from the nose.

Emergencies

Accidents

Injuries sustained in a road accident can be fatal if not handled correctly and promptly. If your dog is struck by an automobile or motorcycle, it is important that you remain calm. Panic on your part will serve only to upset the injured animal and could cause it to thrash around and injure itself even more seriously.

Often an injured animal is panicky and may snap at you. Always muzzle the dog before lifting it to prevent any injury to yourself.

If your dog is unable to move itself, immediately remove it from the street where it could be further injured. In picking up your injured dog, it is critical that you support the body as fully as possible. The less movement of the injured area the better.

Corgis are of a size that the average person can lift and support without too much difficulty. If for some reason you are alone and lifting your dog presents a problem, gently place it on a blanket and carefully slide the blanket to the vehicle that you will use to transport the dog to your veterinarian.

Do not wait to determine the extent of injury. Internal injuries may have occurred that you are unable to observe immediately. Get the injured dog to a veterinarian without delay. Ask someone to drive you there so that you are free to hold your injured dog and keep it calm. If there is no one else available to drive you, put the injured dog in a box or shipping kennel of some kind to keep it as immobile as possible.

Poisoning

If Your Corgi Is Poisoned:

1 Keep the telephone number of your local poison control center with your other emergency numbers.

2 If you know or suspect which poison your dog has ingested, give this information to the poison control center when you call them. They may be able to prescribe an immediate antidote.

3 Have the emergency number of your dog's veterinarian or the nearest 24-hour emergency veterinary hospital current and easily available. Give any information you receive from the poison control center to your veterinarian.

4 If you are not sure that your dog has been poisoned or which poison it may have ingested, describe the symptoms you are observing to your veterinarian.

5 Common symptoms of poisoning:
  ◆ Convulsions
  ◆ Paralysis
  ◆ Tremors
  ◆ Vomiting
  ◆ Diarrhea
  ◆ Stomach cramps and pain, accompanied by whimpering or howling, heavy breathing.

Bleeding Wounds

If there is a bleeding wound due to a traffic accident or any other accident, deal with the bleeding at once. Using a pad of cotton or a compress soaked in cold water, apply pressure directly to the bleeding point. If the flow of blood is not stemmed, your dog could bleed to death.

For a wound on one of the limbs that is severely hemorrhaging and that pressure will not stop, tie a tourniquet above the wound. Even a handkerchief or belt can serve this purpose. If you do use a tourniquet, loosen the pressure every ten minutes or so to avoid having the tissues suffer lack of oxygen.

A Corgi seldom will pick fights with other dogs, but neither will it back down when challenged. Should your dog be injured in a fight, get it to the veterinarian without delay. Bite wounds are invariably infected and antibiotic treatment is necessary.

Stings and Bites

Corgis are curious animals and seem fascinated by all things that fly and crawl. They naturally attempt to examine insects with their paws or mouths. This can lead to bites and stings on the foot, or worse, on or around the mouth or nose.

If the sting is visible, remove it with a pair of tweezers and apply a saline solution or mild antiseptic. If the swelling is large, particularly inside the mouth, or if the dog appears to be in shock, contact your veterinarian at once.

Choking and Foreign Objects

If you notice signs of choking, wedge something between the dog's teeth in the side of the mouth to keep the mouth open and to avoid being bitten. Check the back of the throat, between the teeth, and on the roof of the mouth for foreign objects. Pull the tongue out carefully to see if something has been lodged at the back of it. Use your fingers to try and remove any object you find that is causing the dog to choke.

If you are unable to dislodge the object, hold the dog upside down by grabbing it around the middle just in front of the hips and shake vigorously to help dislodge the object and clear the airway. If this does not work, try applying sudden pressure to the abdomen at the edge of the breastbone using your fist. Even if you do dislodge the article, get your dog to the veterinarian without delay.

Heat Stroke

Allowing a dog to remain in an automobile during hot weather is the most common cause of heat stroke. Signs of panic with excessive panting and disorientation are obvious symptoms as are bright red gums, indications of shock, and vomiting.

In such a case immediately immerse the dog in cold water and, while someone is watching the dog, call your veterinarian at once. Do not wait to see if the dog's condition changes. Get the dog to your veterinarian at once.

Burns

For minor burns apply a cold compress or cold water for 15 minutes. Then apply antibiotic cream and cover with elastic wrap. In the event of a major burn, get your dog to the veterinarian at once.

Illnesses

Rabies

It is important that you are aware of the clinical signs of rabies in animals and report any animal bites to your veterinarian. Generally speaking, there are two types of rabies: the violent type and what is referred to as "dumb rabies." In the violent type the afflicted animal goes wild, biting and attacking anything that moves. An animal with the dumb type of rabies will appear to be paralyzed and may sit staring without focus. The animal's lower jaw may hang open, dribbling saliva.

Rabies shots are normally given when puppies are four to six months old. Again, the possibility of your Corgi coming into contact with undomesticated animals may make earlier immunization a wise choice. Discuss this with your veterinarian.

Kennel Cough

Kennel cough (infectious rhinotracheitis), while highly infectious, is not a serious disease; it is like a mild case of influenza in humans. It is caused by a mixture of a bacteria and a virus. The name of the disease is misleading as it implies that a dog must be in a kennel environment to be infected. Actually, it is very easily passed from one dog to another in almost any situation.

The Corgi gets along well with other dogs, but be sure your pet's inoculations are up-to-date if you plan to take him or her out and about.

The symptoms can make the disease sound far worse than it actually is. They are particularly nerve-racking because there is a persistent hacking cough that at times makes one think that surely the dog will bring up everything it has ever eaten!

Various protective procedures can be administered by your veterinarian. In addition to inoculations, there is an intranasal vaccine available. These protective measures are advisable for your Corgi if you ever take it to a dog park or plan on placing it in a boarding kennel or participate in group obedience classes. Many boarding kennels now insist upon proof of protection against kennel cough before they will allow a dog to be admitted.

Coronavirus

Coronavirus, also referred to as coronaviral gastroenteritis, is a highly contagious virus and can be caused by ingesting fecal matter of an infected canid, which can also include coyotes and foxes. Dogs of any age can be infected and symptoms include watery stools, vomiting, and anorexia. Coronavirus can be successfully treated by a veterinarian but immunization is recommended to prevent the disease.

Internal Parasites

Tapeworms and heartworms are best diagnosed and treated by your veterinarian. Great advances are continually made in dealing with both of these parasites

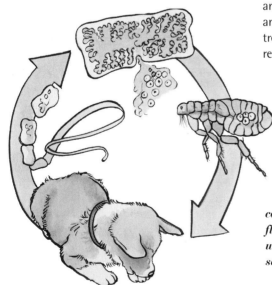

Life cycle of the tapeworm: fleas are commonly hosts of the tapeworm. When a flea is swallowed, the parasite is shared with your dog—tapeworms develop and segments are passed in the feces.

Exercise must be adjusted as your Corgi gets older, and you must be careful that the old-timer is not pushed beyond its capacity when hiking or playing.

and what was once a complicated and time-consuming treatment has been simplified over the years. Most of the dog's internal parasites are readily detected by your veterinarian's microscopic inspection of the dog's stool.

Tapeworms

Tapeworms are a part of the life cycle of the flea. If your dog has fleas now or has had fleas in the past, it undoubtedly has tapeworm. A sign of infection is the appearance of segments of the worm crawling around the dog's anus or in the stool just after the dog has relieved itself. Your veterinarian can inoculate your Corgi if it has this problem, and the tapeworms are quickly and completely eliminated.

Whipworms

Whipworms are round and tapered in shape. These parasites normally settle in the cecum and upper part of the large intestine. They are extremely difficult to see other than by veterinary inspection of the stool. The parasites thrive on the host and can cause severe impairment of the dog's health and, in extreme cases, even death.

Roundworms

Roundworms are not an unusual condition in dogs and are rarely harmful in an adult dog; however, these parasites can cause extreme health hazards to puppies if present in large amounts.

Roundworms can be transmitted from mother to puppies, so make sure that your female is free of roundworms before you breed her.

Hookworms

These tiny parasites attach themselves to the insides of the small intestines. They multiply rapidly and suck the blood of the infected dog. This can be extremely and quickly debilitating to puppies and young dogs. Stool sample examination by a veterinarian is recommended for any dog or puppy that continues to act listless.

Heartworms

Heartworms (also called filariae) are parasitic worms found in dogs' hearts. Dogs are the only mammals that are commonly affected. The worm is transmitted by mosquitoes that carry the larvae of the worm.

Your veterinarian can detect the presence of heartworm by a blood test. There is a preventive medication called Ivermectin, used by veterinarians for a dog that tests negative for the parasite. Dogs that have already been infected can be treated with a relatively new corrective medication called Melarsomine. These medications must be prescribed by a veterinarian; he or she will do so only after taking the appropriate tests.

Inherited Health Problems

In the wild any genetically transferred infirmity that would interfere with any newborn animal's ability to nurse, to capture food as an adult, or to escape from a predator, would automatically eliminate the individual from the gene pool.

We who control the breeding of our domesticated dogs are intent upon saving all the puppies in a litter, but in preserving life we also perpetuate health

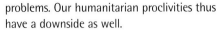

problems. Our humanitarian proclivities thus have a downside as well.

Like all breeds of domesticated dogs, the Corgi has its share of hereditary problems; fortunately the problems are relatively few. The diseases described here will rarely, if ever, be present in the Corgi you buy from a respected breeder, nor are these problems necessarily to be found in your Corgi's immediate ancestors. They are breed problems, however, that should be discussed with the breeder from whom you purchase your dog. As stated previously, the reputable Corgi breeder is aware of the following problems and should be more than willing to discuss them with you.

General Back and Joint Problems

Because of their long backs and short-legged conformation both Corgi breeds are susceptible to back and joint problems. Owners should limit or even eliminate the opportunities for puppies and young dogs to leap on and off chairs or stairs. High-impact games and exercises should be avoided until a Corgi is at least a year old.

Ruptured Disc Syndrome

Although some attribute the ruptured disc syndrome to the fact that the Corgis are long-backed breeds, it appears this is not entirely the case. There are a number of short-backed breeds that are also affected

Heartworms (also called filariae) are parasitic worms found in the hearts of infected dogs. Infected mosquitoes bite a dog and deposit the heartworm larvae on its skin. The larvae enter the bloodstream through the hole created by the mosquito bite and make their way to the dog's heart.

by this same problem, while many other long-backed breeds are not. Thus, it appears this is more likely a matter of individual breed sensitivity and that certain Corgi bloodlines are more prone to this sensitivity than others.

In short, the ruptured disc syndrome is that in which the spongelike disc that acts as a cushion between the spinal vertebrae ruptures. The pressure of this ruptured disc against the spinal column causes extreme pain and, in some cases, partial or complete paralysis of the hindquarters.

Normal activity, including jumping off furniture, will not cause discs to rupture unless the dog is prone to the condition in the first place. Again, this is looked upon as a condition that can be more or less prevalent in some lines and definitely bears being discussed with the breeder of the puppy you are considering.

Hip Dysplasia

Hip dysplasia, commonly referred to as HD, is a developmental disease of the hip joint. One or both hip joints of the affected dog have abnormal contours. Some dogs might show tenderness in the hip, walk with a limp or swaying gait, or experience difficulty getting up. Symptoms vary from mild, temporary lameness to severe crippling in extreme cases. Treatment may require surgery. Even though hip dysplasia is not rampant in the Corgi breeds, enough cases have been reported to merit asking the breeder of your puppy what testing they have done in respect to the problem.

Eye Problems

Both the Cardigan and Pembroke Corgis experience eye problems to a degree that screening has become necessary. Conscientious breeders test all their breeding stock and do

not use animals in their breeding programs that carry the genes for these conditions.

Progressive Retinal Atrophy

This condition, commonly referred to as PRA, is the most common eye disease affecting the two Corgi breeds. It is a degenerative disease of the retinal cells of the eye that progresses to blindness. It usually occurs later in Corgis more than six years old. Fortunately eye testing of breeding stock is now done by responsible breeders. Detecting the "carriers" of PRA and avoiding their use in a breeding program can virtually eliminate the problem.

Secondary Glaucoma

Secondary glaucoma is not entirely uncommon in the Corgi. Glaucoma involves increased pressure within the eye. When the fluid this pressure creates is unable to escape from the eye, the eyeball becomes swollen and painful. This is a congenital condition, but it seldom appears until the dog has fully matured. Again, conscientious breeders are aware of these problems and guard against them with professional screening.

Von Willebrand's Disease

This is an inherited bleeding disorder that is similar to hemophilia but not as severe. It is seldom fatal but it is very important to be aware of in the event surgery is required.

Cystitis

Cystitis is a severe inflammation of the urinary bladder. The affected dog may whine or show other evidence of pain when it urinates. Corgis can be prone to the problem but in a good many cases the condition can be relieved quickly with antibiotics.

SHARING YOUR LIFE WITH A CORGI

Corgi Versatility

Everything in the Corgi's history and genetic makeup tells the same story: This is a working dog. If prospective dog owners are looking for a companion that loves to sit on its owner's lap all day or one that is content to lie patiently in front of the hearth while its owners are away day in and day out, they should consider another breed.

Like nearly all the herding breeds, the Corgi's heritage equips it to think problem situations out and to work the whole day through. Do not expect any Corgi to harness that physical and mental energy and keep it in reserve because its owner would prefer the dog to loll around the house all day without a thing to do. *There is no such thing as a Corgi that has nothing to do!* If a Corgi's owner does not provide the dog with assigned duties, the dog will create its own activity schedule, and what the clever Corgi decides on its own needs doing may not (and probably will not) coincide with what its owner might prefer.

On the other hand, if the prospective owner of a Corgi is a reasonably active person who derives as much pleasure from training a dog as the Corgi derives from being trained, this person

Your Corgi will always be ready for action and fun.

will undoubtedly join the ranks of the thousands of Corgi owners who consider the breed one of the most trainable and intelligent in existence.

If any activity calls for speed, endurance, athletic ability, and intelligence, the Corgi is a great candidate. There is such a wide array of events a Corgi is capable of competing and excelling in that it is highly unlikely that even the most energetic or athletic owner will ever exhaust the Corgi's potential.

What makes a Corgi such a versatile breed is its ability to perform well in a wide array of activities with complete ease. Your Corgi can be a Canine Good Citizen certificate holder, conformation show competitor, obedience trial star, speed demon on the agility course, and herding trial whiz (see pages 96–101)—and this is just scratching the surface of activities in which the Corgi can participate.

With all this said about a Corgi's energy level, the two Corgi breeds have proven time and time again they can also make wonderful therapy dogs for the aged and infirm.

Companions

The wonderful thing about all this is that the more involved and the more proficient your Corgi becomes in any—or for that matter, all—of the above, the better it will become at being your best buddy and companion. While we have said time and again that the Corgi is not a dog for just anyone, we can also say the owner who is suited to this breed could not possibly hope to have a better dog.

It would be impossible to give all the detailed training instructions necessary to make your Corgi proficient in the many activities for which it is suitable. We will, however, attempt to give a broad overview of the activities that many Corgis have excelled in and leave it up to the owners to pursue any of them in which they have an interest. Additional information on these activities can be found on page 124.

Canine Good Citizen Test

The purpose of this test is to demonstrate that the canine entered is well mannered and an asset to the community. There are ten parts to the test and the dog must pass all ten in order to be awarded a certificate:

1 Accepting a Friendly Stranger
2 Sitting Politely for Petting
3 Appearance and Grooming
4 Out for a Walk (Walking on a loose lead)
5 Walking through a Crowd
6 Sit and Down on Command/Staying in Place
7 Coming When Called
8 Reaction to Another Dog
9 Reactions to Distractions
10 Supervised Separation

If the dog successfully completes each of the exercises, it is awarded the Canine Good Citizen title, a certificate is issued by the AKC, and the designation CGC will officially be added after the dog's registered name.

Conformation Shows

Popular and well-attended dog events are the combined conformation shows and obedience trials regulated by the American Kennel Club and the United Kennel Club. The original purpose of conformation shows was to give breeders a means of comparing their stock to that of other fanciers and thereby make improvements in their breeding programs.

Today, not all people who participate in conformation shows intend to become breeders. Many simply find enjoyment in the competitive aspect of these events. Referred to by some as "canine beauty contests," conformation dog shows take place nearly every weekend of the year in one part of the country or another and are open to all non-neutered, AKC- or UKC-registered dogs.

Generally speaking, conformation shows fall into two major categories: matches and championship events. Match shows are primarily staged for the young or inexperienced dogs that are not ready to compete for championship points. In most cases classes are offered for dogs beginning at about three months.

Match Shows

Matches are an excellent place for novice handlers to learn to show their own dogs. Since these match shows are far more informal than championship events, there is plenty of time for the novice handler to ask questions and seek assistance from more experienced exhibitors or from the officiating judges.

Match shows can be held for all breeds or they can be what are referred to as "specialty matches" for one or both Corgis only. When there is a club devoted to a specific breed in an area, that club will often hold these match shows so that the newer club members and the young puppies will have an opportunity to gain some experience.

Information regarding these matches can usually be found in the classified sections of Sunday newspapers under "Dogs for Sale." Local breeders are usually aware of scheduled events of this kind as well.

There is no need to enter these informal matches ahead of time. Most accept entries on the grounds of the show site the morning of the event. The person taking your entry will be able to assist you in filling out the entry form and give you the preliminary instructions you will need.

Championship Shows

Championship shows are much more formal in nature and best entered after you have gained some experience by participating in several match events. Championship shows are sponsored by various all-breed kennel clubs or in some instances by a club specializing in one particular breed of dog. The AKC can provide you with the name of the all-breed kennel club in your area and the national Corgi clubs can let you know if there is a Pembroke or Cardigan Corgi specialty club in your vicinity (see Information, page 124).

For obedience work beyond the basics, there are free classes at parks and recreation facilities as well as very formal individual lessons conducted by private trainers.

How a Champion Is Made

A registered dog can become a champion of record by winning 15 championship points. These points are awarded to the best male and best female nonchampions in each breed. The number of championship points that can be won at a particular show is based upon the number of entries in a dog's own breed and sex entered at the show and the area in which the show is located. These requirements are determined by the organization sponsoring the event, primarily the AKC or UKC.

Catalogs sold at all AKC championship shows list the particulars relevant to every dog entered in the show: the dog's name, its sire and dam, its date of birth, and the names of its breeder and owner.

The catalog also tells the number of dogs required to win points in each breed. Since the number of dogs necessary to win points differs geographically, it is important to check the catalog at every show in which your dog competes to find the number of points it might win.

Trials and Events

Obedience

Obedience trials are held at both championship shows and matches, as are the conformation events. The same informal entry procedures that apply to conformation matches apply here as well. The championship or "sanctioned" obedience trials are normally held in conjunction with conformation events and normally require pre-entry.

Obedience training classes are definitely prerequisites here, since competition is highly precise and based entirely upon your dog's performing a set series of exercises. The exercises required in the various classes of competition range from basics like *heel, sit,* and *down* in the novice class on through the sophisticated exercises of the utility and tracking dog levels that require scent discrimination and directed jumping.

Each level has a title that can be earned after attaining qualifying scores at a given number of shows. The competition levels and corresponding degrees are:

◆ Novice, earning a Companion Dog degree (CD)

◆ Open, earning the Companion Dog Excellent degree (CDX)

◆ Utility, earning the Utility Dog and Utility Dog Excellent degrees (UD and UDX)

Many people find that the competitive aspect of dog shows provides a great deal of fun and excitement as well as a pleasant diversion from an average work week.

Obedience and Agility trials challenge dog and owner to work as a team, and strengthen the bond between them.

Those "super dogs" who have earned their Utility Dog titles are eligible to go on to compete for the next highest award—the Obedience Trial Championship (OTCh).

Tracking events have become very popular among Corgi owners and earn the rare Tracking Dog and Tracking Dog Excellent titles (TD and TDX). A newer competition called Variable Surface Tracking (VST) is open to the dogs that have won their TD or TDX titles. When the competitors in this category have attained the qualifying scores they earn the VST designation.

Agility

Agility competition is actually an obstacle course for dogs. Everyone involved (and everyone who watches) appears to be having the time of their lives. There are 14 obstacles that the canine contestants must master off-leash while being timed. The course includes tunnels, cat walks, seesaws, hoops, and numerous other obstacles. Still in the early stages of growth, this event is catching on rapidly and will undoubtedly become one of the biggest attractions at all breed dog shows.

Herding Tests and Trials

Many Corgi breeders encourage those who purchase puppies from them to participate in herding events because they believe the trials help preserve and perpetuate the breed's herding instincts.

Herding trials are sponsored by several organizations including the American Herding Breeds Association (AHBA). Requirements and titles differ slightly from one organization to the next but generally produce the same results. Details can be obtained directly from these organizations.

The AKC's events are open to dogs over nine months of age that are registered with the organization as a herding breed. There are three levels of competition involved in the AKC's program: Herding Test, Pretrial Test, and Herding Trials.

Herding test: This test is quite simple as it is designed to reveal the dog's willingness to respond to its handler and its ability to control the movement of the livestock involved—cattle, goats, sheep, or even ducks.

In order to pass the test the dog must successfully accomplish the following:

1. Execute a *stay* on command.

2. Follow two commands to change the direction of the moving stock.

3. Stop on command.

4. Come on recall.

Ten minutes are allowed for the exercises. The dog must successfully pass two such tests under two different judges and no score is given; the test is either passed or failed. After passing both tests the participating dog is awarded the Herding Tested degree (HT), which becomes an official title and can be added to its registered name.

Pretrial test: Once earned, the HT degree makes the dog eligible for the Pretrial test. In this event the dog must:

1. Work the livestock through obstacles.

2. Stop the stock.

3. Turn the stock.

4. Reverse the direction of the stock.

5. Pen the stock within ten minutes.

This is also a pass or fail event that must be successfully completed under two different judges and earns the official Pretrial Tested (PT) title.

Herding trial: Dogs competing in the herding trial events have three options in which to compete designated as the A, B, or C course. The three courses are designed to show different areas of working ability.

Each of the courses has three levels of accomplishment: Herding Started (HS), Herding Intermediate (HI), and Herding Advanced (HA). Proficiency in the advanced level earns the dog a Herding Excellent (HX)

Corgis excel at the Flyball events held in many parts of the country. This is a race in which two teams of four dogs race over hurdles to trigger a box that releases a ball that they carry back over the hurdles.

title that is the highest degree attainable by a herding dog.

All of these trials must be completed with a score of at least 60 out of a possible 100 points, which are divided into six categories of proficiency. A dog must earn at least half of the points allotted to each of the six categories in order to qualify.

The courses involve complex patterns, many of which require a participating dog to respond to hand signals from the handler rather than to verbal commands. Details of these complex trials can be obtained from the AKC's Herding Department and there are numerous books and periodicals on the subject listed in the last chapter of this book. The AKC also sponsors herding trial clinics at various locations throughout the United States throughout the year.

Fun and Games

Your Corgi will play games far longer than you may want to, but it is certainly a way in which you can both stay fit and you can help release some of your dog's stored-up energy.

Frisbee: Most Corgis will retrieve a frisbee for hours on end. There are competitions and even national championships offered for dogs excelling in the sport.

Flyball: Flyball is a race in which two teams of four dogs race over hurdles to trigger a box that releases a ball that they carry back over the hurdles. The Corgi is a star at this event.

Hiking: The dedicated outdoors person could not possibly have a better companion than the Corgi. The breed will enjoy hiking as much as any human and its human companion does not have the worry of the Corgi wandering off and disappearing for hours on end; the Corgi wants to be with its owner—*always*.

Your Aging Athlete

The Corgi ages remarkably well, and though lifespan does vary from dog to dog, it is not the least bit unusual to find many members of this breed alive and active as old as 12 and 14 years of age. Some oldtimers maintain their sight and hearing and all their teeth until their final days!

Exercise: Naturally there are certain precautions that must be taken with older Corgis to keep them happy and healthy. Exercise must be adjusted as your dog gets older, and you must take pains to see that your Corgi is not pushed beyond its limits when hiking, playing, or competing in some of the events described. This is especially so if there are any signs of arthritis and if exercise makes your old friend limp. Elderly Corgis might exert themselves beyond what is reasonable just to please you.

Adjusting the diet: As long as your Corgi remains active, no major changes need be made in the dog's diet with the exception of reducing the fat content of the food. Doing so will make the diet easier to digest.

Today, most major dog food manufacturers take canine aging into consideration and offer diets specifically formulated for the senior citizen. Your veterinarian can advise you.

If your Corgi has been accustomed to one major meal each day it is probably wise to adjust the oldtimer's diet to two or three smaller meals. No dog should ever be allowed to become overweight but it is particularly important to avoid obesity in the aging Corgi. The strain of additional weight can affect the Corgi's long back and can certainly shorten its lifespan. There is no reason for this to occur if dog and owner continue to pursue a normal range of activities, albeit with moderation.

BREEDING

As mentioned previously, there is a serious pet overpopulation problem in the United States; therefore, a Corgi owner should think long and hard before making yet another contribution to this critical situation.

Pembroke Corgi rescue organizations are constantly being alerted to Corgis that have found their way into animal shelters across America. This is far less apt to be true in the case of the Cardigan Corgi because so few puppies are sold each year, but even at that, there are rescue cases reported. Many of the rescued animals were born into good homes but obviously fell into the hands of irresponsible buyers.

Breeding Stock

Another factor to consider is the suitability of your female, or for that matter your male, for breeding. As previously discussed, not all Corgis, even though well bred, are suitable as breeding stock. If you expressed your future desire to breed Corgis with the person from whom you purchased your first dog, the breeder will have undoubtedly selected a pup for you that was worthy of perpetuating the breed.

The breeder who brought this little fellow into the world is responsible for him all his life.

Finding the Right Breeder

If the breeder from whom you purchased your Corgi sold the dog to you as pet quality only, it is most likely he or she had no desire to have it bred and you should respect that experienced person's wishes. If you are unable to get in touch with the breeder, or if you doubt the credentials of the person from whom you purchased your dog, do some research and find a local breeder who has the reputation for producing show-quality Corgis. This is the best person to advise you on whether or not your male or female should be bred.

They'll Never Miss It

All too often people who have purchased purebred pets will say to me "Molly needs to have a litter to complete her development" or "Drover needs a girlfriend to relieve his frustration." I assure you, neither Molly nor Drover needs sex to make life complete. Actually, in the case of Drover or any other male, breeding will serve to increase his frustration rather than relieve it.

Now Take Care of Them!

Even if your Corgi is of the quality that warrants reproducing, there are consequences that must be considered. Molly's litter can easily bring a household's dog population to half a dozen overnight. This can be great fun for the entire family for the first couple of weeks when the puppies spend their lives nursing and sleeping. The day will come very quickly, however, when Molly will look at you as if to say "Well, you wanted puppies—now take care of them!"

All too soon the puppies will not only want liberation from the whelping box, they will want to be with you—*all the time!* Think back on the difficulty you experienced in house-training and training a single Corgi puppy. Now multiply that by five or six and consider the cleanup involved for five or six.

You must realize the commitment you will have to make to being on hand when weaning time comes. Newly weaned puppies need four meals a day. Will you or a responsible member of the family be on hand to feed morning, noon, evening, and night?

Corgi puppies must have continuous human contact from birth on if they are to achieve their potential as companions. You must ask yourself if you are willing to give them all the time they need and deserve until you have found a good, responsible home for each puppy in the litter. This may take weeks, sometimes months, after you have already decided it is time for the puppies to be off to their new homes.

Problems with Males

Males that have been used for breeding may have an extremely difficult time keeping themselves from lifting their leg and marking their territory. A male's territory will include everything in your home from new draperies to an antique sofa. Then, too, breeding seems to awaken the *machismo* instinct in male Corgis. Some stud dogs can become a handful when you are trying to keep them from continually proving they are the toughest kid on the block.

Financial Considerations

Some individuals are willing to commit to all of the above in anticipation of financial gain. They multiply the selling price of a hypothetical number of puppies by somewhere in the area of $500–$600 and think, "Wow, what a great source of income!"

Think again! Stop to consider the cost of a stud fee and prenatal veterinary expenses, then add the cost of possible whelping problems, health checks, and the necessary inoculation series for the puppies. These are all significant cost factors that must be taken into consideration and they are the same factors that will put a very large dent in any anticipated profits.

When the Answer Is "Yes"

If what we have written thus far has not discouraged you and you have decided you really want to raise a litter of Corgis, you must begin to plan well ahead. Responsible breeding is not a matter of tossing your female into the back seat of your car and heading for the nearest male of the same breed.

Helpful hint: If this is your first litter, something worth considering is that a summer litter is infinitely easier to care for than one born and growing up during seasons when the weather is inclement. It is much easier to fence off a good-sized area outdoors than to find equal space inside the home. Growing Corgi puppies need space to exercise and stretch those rapidly growing muscles. The freedom to put what we refer to as our "wrecking crews" safely outdoors during the summer months has proven to be a godsend, and the puppies seem to love it as well.

Think your planning through carefully. Your female will not whelp until approximately two months after she is bred. The puppies will thus spend the first three or four weeks after they are born in their whelping box; it is during the following eight or twelve weeks that you will welcome good weather.

Health Checks

No Corgi female should ever be bred until you are sure that she has had at least two heat cycles or is at least two years old. Before this time, she is not completely mature mentally or physically. You must be sure she is in good health and is not a carrier for the breed's hereditary problems. Some tests such as those for hip dysplasia require X rays. Eye problems are usually diagnosed by specialists in the field. Your veterinarian can assist you in determining whether any hereditary conditions exist.

All dogs—male and female—must be tested for canine brucellosis before being bred. This is one of the few venereal diseases that afflict dogs. It is a bacterial infection transmitted sexually and through a dog's saliva. It is one cause of abortion in females and of male sterility.

Average Costs Involved in Raising a Litter of Five Corgi Puppies to Eight to Ten Weeks of Age

Cost of breeding quality female	$ 1000.00
Pre-breeding veterinary examination including brucellosis test	75.00
Stud fee	600.00
Prenatal costs, whelping box, gauze pads, heating pad, emergency supplemental feeder, mother's milk replacement, rectal thermometer, sterilized scissors, cotton thread, lubricant, baby scale, infrared lamp	200.00
Post-whelping veterinary examination (dam and puppies)	75.00
Tail/dewclaw docking	125.00
Time lost from work	300.00
Inoculations (three-shot series for each puppy)	350.00
Advertising	150.00
Food costs (mother and puppies)	200.00
	$ 3075.00
Possible cesarean delivery	$ 850.00
	$ 3925.00

Note: Most potential buyers of puppies are inclined to go to an established breeder if they are looking for a female to breed or show. First-time breeders are most likely to attract customers who are interested in obtaining a pet-quality puppy at an average cost of about $500.

These tests for hereditary health problems also apply to your male if he is to be used at stud. Again, we urge the owner of a male to consider the consequences of using the dog for breeding, even once.

Approaches to Breeding

There are three different ways of mating purebred animals of any kind. They are referred to as *inbreeding, outcrossing,* and *linebreeding.* The genetic inheritance of the litter your Corgi female will produce depends upon the relationship of the individuals in her pedigree and the pedigree of the stud dog you eventually select.

Inbreeding

This is an attempt to fix certain mental and physical characteristics in the offspring by mating closely related individuals. Breedings between mother and son, father and daughter, and brother and sister are examples of inbreeding. Inbreeding fixes both qualities and faults;

Summer litters are infinitely easier to care for than puppies born during a season of inclement weather.

therefore, it is a method that should be resorted to only by experienced Corgi breeders

Outcrossing

Outcrossing is the opposite of inbreeding. This method of breeding mates individuals that, for all intents and purposes, are not related but are of the same breed. This approach is less likely to fix faults in the offspring, but neither can it concentrate specific qualities with any certainty.

Linebreeding

This might be considered the happy medium between inbreeding and outcrossing and is the method by which most quality Corgis are produced. Related animals are used but the common ancestor or ancestors may be two or three

Corgis have a long-standing history of amiable temperament and suitability for both adult and child.

generations removed. Linebreeding affords the same benefits and drawbacks of inbreeding, but to a lesser degree.

The Stud Dog

The decision to breed your female was based upon the fact that she is of the quality and temperament that make her a likely candidate to produce worthy offspring. This does not mean she is a perfect Corgi by any stretch of the imagination. No dog of any breed is perfect—not even the greatest show winner. The likelihood of your female Corgi having no faults to compensate for in selecting a stud dog is extremely remote. The stud dog you select should excel in those areas in which your female has shortcomings, but above all he must have a sound and stable temperament. Responsible Corgi breeders must never settle for anything less.

The Corgi male advertised in the newspaper or owned by an acquaintance may carry none of the compensating qualities your female needs in her offspring. Far more dangerous to future offspring, an irresponsibly chosen mate for your female might conceivably carry faults in his genetic makeup that, added to those in your female's genes, will create serious problems. For instance: doubling up on the genes that produce unreliable temperament may produce aggressive or extremely shy offspring, even though the male and female used appear to be sound and stable.

The breeder of your female will be familiar with the pedigree, conformation, and tempera-

ment—all the assets and shortcomings of the line of Corgis from which your female descends. Your breeder will also be the best person to advise you on which faults your female has that the proper stud dog should be able to compensate for.

If the breeder of your female is not available for some reason, both the Pembroke Welsh Corgi Club of America and the Cardigan Welsh Corgi Club of America maintain lists of responsible breeders. You may be able to select someone from these lists who lives nearby and who can offer sound advice regarding the proper selection of a stud dog.

Agreements and Fees

Paperwork

The owner of a stud dog should be able to present proof that care and testing indicates the stud dog is not a carrier of the hereditary problems of the breed. You should be able to provide proof of your female's physical and genetic health as well.

The stud dog owner will be able to provide you with a four-generation pedigree of his or her dog. You should also bring a copy of your female's pedigree when you first go to see the stud dog. The owner of the stud will be anxious to see if your female's bloodlines will be compatible with those of the stud. You can also ask the owner of the stud how to go about arranging to have the forthcoming litter registered.

Stud Fee

The cost of breeding to the male you select (the stud fee) should be determined in advance as well. Stud fees vary depending upon the male's proven ability to produce quality puppies. The cost of breeding to a young male that has yet to produce a litter is going to be much less than that of a male that has produced many champion offspring. The predictability of what kind of offspring the unproven male will be able to produce is also significantly less.

The stud fee is always payable at the time of breeding and is payment for breeding your female to the designated male—nothing more; it is not a guarantee of living puppies.

Breeding Agreement

Any agreements and conditions outside of a guarantee of actual mating should be clearly outlined in a stud contract or breeding agreement. This agreement should list the amount of the stud fee and any special conditions that apply. For instance, there are times when the owner of the stud must resort to artificial means to insure a breeding. The cost involved in this process may be additional to the negotiated stud fee.

If the female is to remain on the premises of the stud owner while she is being bred, the contract should also state what additional costs are involved in keeping her there. The contract should state what the owner of the stud dog is responsible for while the female is in residence.

Pick of the Litter

On occasion, the owner of a Corgi stud dog will agree to have his or her dog mate your female in return for first choice of the resulting puppies. This can be a good arrangement for those who do not plan on keeping a puppy from the litter for themselves. If the owner of the female plans to keep a pup from the litter to show or to breed or for any other reason, this option should be considered carefully. It is extremely difficult to give up the puppy you had grown attached to or planned to keep as a show prospect, even when you have agreed to do so beforehand.

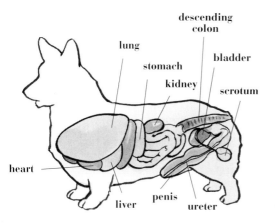

Internal organs of the male Welsh Corgi.

Internal organs of the female Welsh Corgi.

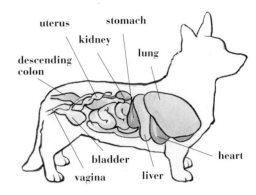

Breeding Reservation

Once the stud dog has been decided upon, the owner of the female should make a breeding reservation based upon the regularity of the female's previous seasons. This will give the owner of a popular stud dog the opportunity to schedule other females that may be coming in to breed to the dog of your choice.

The Heat Cycle

The female can be bred only at a particular time during her heat cycle, which lasts approximately 21 days. Most females will normally come into heat, called *estrus*, for the first time at about ten to twelve months of age; it can take place as early as six months. After her first heat, your female will be in heat again fairly regularly every six to eight months.

A noticeable swelling of the vulva, followed in a few days by a dark bloody vaginal discharge, are the first signs that your female is in heat. Once you have noticed this, she should be watched very carefully and kept away from all males to avoid any accidental matings. She should also be confined to an area of the household where the discharge, which she is unable to control, will not soil carpeting or furniture.

If your female is to be bred at this season, you should at once notify the owner of the stud dog you have chosen. The owner of the stud dog can then schedule the breeding and tell you when to arrive with your female.

It is commonly accepted that females of almost all breeds are not ready to accept the male until about the tenth day of their heat cycle. Do not, however, allow that information to lull you into believing that your Corgi *cannot* be bred before or after that time. While desired matings seldom are accomplished prior to the tenth day of the heat cycle, it seems *unwanted* matings are productive at almost any time the female is in heat.

Timing Is Critical

A veterinarian can be extremely helpful in advising the right day on which to breed your female. Blood tests and vaginal smears can be performed that will determine just when the female's ovulation has begun and the right time to have her bred.

Even though your female has been successfully mated to the dog of your choice, do not assume she cannot be impregnated by another dog. She must be closely watched until she has completely ended her heat cycle. Litters can be produced that have had two or more entirely different sires, one a purebred Corgi, the other a dog of mixed parentage. Should this unfortunate situation occur it does not mean that your female is "tainted" for life. Her subsequent litters will not be affected in any way if she is properly mated and watched.

PREGNANCY; WHELPING AND RAISING PUPPIES

Is She or Isn't She?

There is nothing unusually different you need do for your female Corgi for the first four or five weeks after she has been bred; maintain her normal schedule and diet. There is no reason to restrict the amount of exercise she has been used to. In fact, maintaining good muscle tone will serve her well when whelping actually occurs.

We know we cannot tell if one of our females has become pregnant for several weeks after she has been bred. Still, we invariably lapse into what we call our staring mode. While caught up in this phase we gaze intently at the mother-to-be, noting any little sign that will indicate that she is or is not pregnant. We change our minds daily, sometimes hourly, but in the end we must wait about five weeks when a swelling of the female's teats will indicate that the breeding has apparently taken.

Preparations

The Whelping Box

The gestation period is normally 59 to 63 days, which gives you plenty of time to be well prepared for the birth of the litter.

This Corgi dam is her puppy's first teacher; but soon its owner will assume the duties of "pack leader."

The whelping box can be made from a cardboard shipping carton or constructed of wood. Our suggestion would be to purchase or build a box constructed of wood, as the puppies will continue to use it as their bed even after they have been weaned. As the puppies grow, you will find them leaving the whelping box to relieve themselves, thus assisting you in the first stages of their house-training.

The box should be approximately 30 inches (76 cm) square with sides about 10 inches (25 cm) high. The box need not be covered, but if it is, the top should be high enough to allow the mother to stand upright and at least one side should be low enough to allow the female easy access. Whelping boxes of various shapes and sizes can be obtained at most pet supply stores, or if carpentry is your long suit, a whelping box can easily be constructed of inexpensive, well-sanded wood.

The important thing is that your female should be able to hop in and out of the whelping box easily without injuring her puppies, Once in, she should be able to stretch out fully on her side so that all of her teats will be available for the puppies to nurse on. Keep the bottom of the whelping box lined with several layers of newspaper or unprinted newspaper stock that can be obtained at most printing shops and will keep mother and puppies much cleaner looking.

Prenatal Care

As previously mentioned, there is little different that must be done for the first several weeks of pregnancy. If the female has been fed a nutritious, well-balanced diet, you need only continue doing so.

At about the fifth week of her pregnancy her appetite will increase and you may begin to add to the amount of food she is receiving. Do not overfeed, and do not feel she must be given special food or treats; you should avoid allowing the pregnant female to become too fat as obesity can create serious problems at whelping time. Since the female's abdomen is already crowded, several smaller meals during the course of the day will be more beneficial than allowing her to gorge herself once or twice a day.

Standby Whelping Equipment
◆ Whelping box
◆ Newsprint or newspaper
◆ Toweling
◆ Gauze pads
◆ Small box with adjustable heating pad
◆ Emergency supplemental feeder
◆ Mother's milk replacement
◆ Glucose
◆ Rectal thermometer
◆ Disposable rubber gloves
◆ Blunt sterilized scissors
◆ Cotton thread
◆ Lubricant
◆ Scale
◆ Infrared lamp
◆ Patience!
◆ Telephone numbers: Veterinarian's or 24-hour emergency clinics

Some dog owners feel that megadoses of vitamins are necessary during pregnancy. This is definitely not so. In fact, many experienced breeders now feel that large doses of vitamins are dangerous because, improperly administered, there can be long-range detrimental effects on the puppies' skeletal development. It must be remembered that the vast majority of commercial dog foods are highly fortified to begin with, so adding high concentrations of additional vitamins without careful consideration can create problems.

Your veterinarian can advise you when and if any vitamins or medications are necessary. Veterinarians should also be told of your female's pregnancy prior to treatment of any kind, as no inoculations should be given that will affect the normal growth of the fetuses she is carrying.

Whelping the Litter

As the time draws near for the actual whelping, it is wise to assemble the items that will assist you in insuring that the delivery will go smoothly.

Ordinarily, whelping a Corgi litter progresses with few complications. The breed is basically healthy with none of the abnormal breed points that make whelping difficult in some other breeds. Most Corgi females whelp their own puppies naturally with little assistance from their owners.

Even first-time mothers sever the umbilical cord and clean the puppies without any assistance. The owner's only duty is to stand by with a watchful eye just in case complications arise.

Whelping a litter for the first time usually proves to be more traumatic for the owner than

for the dog. Mother Nature has provided your Corgi with a whole set of instinctive behaviors that will take place when the proper time comes. On the very rare occasion that your female does not respond properly or that you suspect something is wrong, call your veterinarian. A veterinarian is trained to know what to do and when to do it. Why should you try to guess your way along when years of study and experience are as accessible as your telephone?

When the Female Starts to Whelp

It is wise to be completely prepared for the female to start whelping at least a week before the time she is actually due. Some females are a few days early, others a few days late. If one of our females is running late we usually take her to our veterinarian just to make sure there are no complications. We have had an occasional female whelp as much as a week late

Ordinarily, whelping a Corgi litter progresses with few complications. Most Corgi females whelp their own puppies naturally with little assistance from their owners.

with no difficulties, but it is best to be sure there are no complications.

This is not the time to allow your female to be outdoors alone. You cannot imagine how inventive some Corgi mothers-to-be can become in finding a little den under the house or some other inaccessible place to whelp her puppies. It can and does happen. Keep her in or near her whelping box as much as possible.

The female's temperature will usually drop from a normal 101.5°F (38.6°C) to 99°F (37.2°C) within 48 hours of the time she will begin whelping. This is often accompanied by general restlessness, shivering, and panting.

There will often be a clear mucous discharge from the vulva that will act as a lubricant during the whelping process. The female will begin scratching in her whelping box, preparing a "nest" in which to deposit her puppies. Some females will vomit during this stage.

These signs can continue for up to 24 hours before contractions actually commence. Although it is obvious the female is experiencing discomfort, there is no need to be unduly concerned unless she appears to be in pain.

Uterine contractions increase in frequency and intensity and the vulva and vagina slowly begin to dilate. Often, the laboring mother will swing around to investigate her rear end and then lie down, stretching her rear legs to press against the sides of the whelping box or squat and strain as if she is trying to relieve her bowels. She may howl or whimper during these contractions.

If contractions continue and no puppies arrive during the next two hours you should definitely seek the advice of your veterinarian. In some cases a puppy is too large to be passed naturally and a cesarean section may be needed.

The First Puppy Arrives

The first puppy is usually preceded by a water bag that breaks and serves as a warning that a puppy is about to be whelped. After a few minutes and more contractions, the first puppy will work its way along the birth canal and begin to emerge from the vulva, usually head first. Once the head has emerged, the female may rest a moment or two before expelling the rest of the whelp. It will be contained in a membrane sac sometimes connected by the umbilical cord to the placenta.

The puppy must be removed from the sac either by the mother or by you. Normally, the mother immediately gets to work and does all that is necessary, breaking open the sac, biting through the umbilical cord, and licking the puppy until it gives out a loud cry.

If There Is a Problem

On a rare occasion, a female whelping her first litter may seem to be totally surprised by the arrival of her first puppy and, lacking the maternal instinct, will only look at it in amazement. It is then time for you to act. If the puppy remains in the sac it will drown and die.

Break open the membrane at the puppy's head and grasp the umbilical cord about 2 inches (5 cm) from the abdomen, draining the fluid in the cord toward the puppy. Immediately sever the cord at this point with the sterilized scissors. Rub the puppy vigorously with rough toweling to stimulate circulation.

It is wise to make sure that the puppy's nose and throat are clear of mucus at this time. Support the puppy in the palm of one hand with its head toward your fingers. Cover and hold the puppy securely with your other hand. Raise your arms above your head and swing the puppy downward in an arc. The centrifugal force will expel any fluids remaining in the nasal or throat passages. Newborn puppies are far less fragile than most people imagine, so do not be afraid to be vigorous in stimulating the newborn whelp. Use a drop of disinfectant to sterilize the cut end of the umbilical cord still attached to the puppy.

Some Corgi puppies are slow to start breathing. If the mother does not see to this immediately take the puppy away, rub it vigorously, and follow the above procedure to remove any fluid from the lungs. Once you are sure the pup is breathing regularly on its own, you may return it to its mother.

If the placenta has not been expelled along with the puppy, the female will normally do so shortly after the puppy is born. There is one placenta for every puppy born and they must each be accounted for. The mother instinctively wants to eat the placentas and we allow her to have one, because the placenta contains useful nutrients. However, allowing her to eat them all can lead to severe diarrhea, so we quickly remove the rest as they are passed, wrap them in newspaper, and place them in the trash.

Breech Births

Barring unforeseen circumstances, the puppies will usually follow each other in irregular succession. Corgi litters can vary in number from two or three to as high as six or seven puppies. There is no need to be concerned if the female takes time out to rest between births. If she continues to strain and no puppies are passed, consult your veterinarian.

Normally, puppies are born head first, but there is an occasional breech birth in which the puppy is born hind legs first. There is no real need to worry about this, because as we previously stated there are no structural exaggerations in the Corgi that in themselves would

When the mother's birth contractions resume, remove the previously born puppies and place them in a small box right next to the whelping box. On the bottom of the box is a not-too-hot water bottle or heating pad covered with towels.

lead to difficult whelping. Breech births in large-headed breeds like Bulldogs, Boston Terriers, and others can be difficult, because the head of the puppy may not be easily passed.

We gently assist breech births if it appears necessary, and especially if the breech occurs further along in the whelping process. At this point, the female may be tired and the contractions not as strong. In this case, all that needs to be done is to firmly grasp as much of the portion of the puppy as has emerged. As the contractions occur, simultaneously ease the puppy out. It is important to have a firm grasp on as much of the puppy's body as possible when you do this. Do not pull sharply, as you risk injuring the mother. Should you be unable to dislodge the puppy in this manner after ten to fifteen minutes, consult your veterinarian.

After Whelping

Once a puppy has been dried and is breathing properly, we allow it to nurse on the mother until contractions begin again. You will be amazed at the vigor of the newborn Corgi whelps and how quickly they find their mother's milk bar and commence nursing.

Some puppies' ears stand up before others' do.

It is only the rare Corgi puppy that needs to be guided to its mother's teat or given assistance to nurse. More often than not it is a case of insuring that the larger, stronger puppies do not push their smaller littermates out of the way and keep them from getting their fair share of milk.

When the mother's birth contractions resume, we remove the previously born puppies and place them in a small box right next to the whelping box so the female can see that her puppies are safe as she prepares to give birth to the next one. On the bottom of the small box we place a not-too-hot water bottle covered in towels. This will keep the puppies warm while they are away from the mother. It is crucial that newborn and nursing puppies not become chilled, as their temperature-regulating systems are not fully functional at this stage.

We keep water available for the female and also a bowl of broth or milk kept at room temperature throughout the whelping process.

Once whelping has been completed and we have cleaned up the whelping box, we offer the nursing mother light food, such as chicken and rice or even scrambled eggs.

Water and Food

Make sure the mother has plenty to drink at all times from this point on. She must not become dehydrated.

The female's appetite will begin to increase significantly within a day or two and she should be fed several times a day, giving her as much as she wants to eat. Her regular nourishing meals should be resumed and supplemented with meaty soups and thick broths. We usually switch to puppy chow in place of the regular adult kibble, because there are more nutrients in these special formulas.

Veterinary Checkup

Retaining a placenta can cause serious infection. If you suspect one has been retained, mention this to your veterinarian when you take the mother and puppies in for their first checkup. It is wise to have this checkup performed within 24 hours of whelping to avoid any complications and to make sure the mother has not retained any puppies. The veterinarian will also inspect the puppies at this time to make sure there are no abnormalities.

This is the time when the puppies' dewclaws should be removed and the tails of the Pembroke Corgi are docked. Some Pembroke Corgis are born with very short tails but *the Cardigan Corgi's tail is never docked!*

Docking the Tail

Removal of dewclaws is standard procedure for most breeds but not all veterinarians are familiar with tail docking for the Pembroke Corgi. It is customary to dock the Pembroke Corgi's tail so that no tail "stump" remains. Even the puppies that are born with short tails should have the stump removed so that it will not detract from the clean line of the back when the puppy has matured.

The tail should be docked at the exact junction of the tail with the body and on a line flush with the contour of the rump. It is important that the veterinarian who will perform this procedure understands just how the Pembroke tail is docked and if he or she has any questions at all regarding the procedure it might be wise to put the veterinarian in

Keep your puppies healthy with regular visits to the veterinarian.

Be sure the new mother drinks plenty of water so she does not dehydrate.

touch with a breeder who has long-standing experience in this area.

Many breeders dock tails themselves. A popular method is rubber-band docking. Those who use this method feel it is cleaner and causes less discomfort to the puppy than using a knife or shears. The banded tails shrivel and fall off within three to five days. This is not a method for the novice to attempt without instruction from an experienced breeder; however, observing the breeder band the tails on a litter or two should prepare the new breeder to do so as well.

Peace and Quiet

Other than the important trip to the veterinarian, the mother and puppies should be given as much peace and quiet as possible. Undoubtedly, everyone in the household, if not the entire neighborhood, will want to see the puppies, but the mother wants and deserves privacy. Many diseases can be carried from one household to another on clothing and shoes. Young puppies are extremely vulnerable at their early age and it is best not to let anyone outside of the immediate household touch the youngsters.

Mother Corgis are very protective of their offspring and strangers coming and going can be upsetting. It is not beyond an otherwise calm and friendly Corgi mother to greet people she does not know well with a threatening growl at this time.

What the new mother needs is privacy and allowing her this opportunity will permit her to settle in with the important duties of motherhood. Warmth and sustenance are primarily what young puppies require. A constant flow of strangers upsets the mother and disturbs the puppies.

Complications

Corgi mothers are not generally prone to post-whelping complications, but occasionally problems do develop. It is important to be aware of the symptoms to avoid serious complications.

Mastitis

An inflammation of the mammary glands usually associated with bacterial infections, the infection is introduced via the bloodstream through a skin lesion or through the teat canal.

An excess of milk in the female can also cause the breasts to become hard and painful. This is common when nursing females have only one or two puppies and too much milk, with some nipples hardly used. Examine the breasts regularly and massage them gently if milk is building up. If your female seems to be in pain or if one or more glands seem excessively red or hot to the touch, call your veterinarian at once.

Eclampsia

This is a much more serious condition but far less common than mastitis. It is caused by a shortage of calcium in the bloodstream. It may occur just before or any time after whelping, but usually at about three to four weeks after the puppies are born. Symptoms are the mother's extreme restlessness, often along with shivering and vomiting. Her legs or entire body can go stiff, and convulsions may occur. Veterinary treatment must be sought at once. Massive injections of calcium are usually administered and recovery is normally rapid, but the mother should not be returned to her litter, as she will undoubtedly relapse.

Metritis

Metritis is an inflammation of the uterus, and is usually the result of contamination entering the uterus during whelping, or from a retained placenta, or sometimes as a result of bacterial contamination during mating. Fever, abdominal pain, discharge from the vulva, and straining may be seen. Veterinary care is essential to treat this condition.

Pyometra

Pyometra is not directly related to the birth process but occurs between heat periods. Bacteria in the resting uterus multiply and the resulting infection fills the uterus with pus. The bitch often exhibits depression, a fever, and there may be a bloody or foul-smelling discharge from the vulva. In some cases there may be no discharge, but the uterus may be swollen and the abdomen tender. Advanced cases are very serious and may be life-threatening. This condition can be treated only by a veterinarian, and surgery that ends in having the female spayed may be necessary.

Caring for the Puppies

Hand-rearing

It is a rare situation in which a Corgi mother cannot take care of her own puppies, but sometimes a puppy or an entire litter will have to be given supplemental feedings or be completely hand-raised. There are a number of reasons that this may be necessary. At times, there are individual puppies in the litter that are too weak to obtain the necessary amount of milk to maintain optimum growth, or the mother may not be able to nurse any of her puppies because of complications of one sort or another.

Warmth and regular feedings every two hours are critical here. A constant temperature of 85°F (29°C) can be controlled with an infrared lamp suspended above the whelping box.

We keep mother's milk replacement and all the necessary feeding apparatus on hand

There are times when a weak puppy or an entire litter must be given supplemental feedings or be completely hand-raised. Average-size newborn Corgi puppies can be fed with a human baby's bottle.

before whelping day, just in case assistance must be given. Veterinarians are probably the best source of these items and you can get necessary instructions on how to hand-feed should you have to do so.

It is very important to follow all instructions from your veterinarian and those on the feeding product container. A puppy's digestive system is very delicate and can easily be upset, causing diarrhea, dehydration, and even death.

There are many different methods used by breeders and recommended by veterinarians that can be used for supplemental feeding. Discuss this issue with your veterinarian, who can not only provide you with any equipment you might need, but also give you instructions on how to properly proceed with hand-rearing or supplementing for one puppy or an entire litter.

Bottle-feeding

For average-size newborn Corgi puppies, use a human baby's bottle with a baby-sized nipple

for hand-feeding. The puppies will learn to use these nipples quite easily. Puppies that nurse naturally on their mother suck far more than just the nipple itself into their mouths; therefore, they have little or no trouble using the baby bottle method.

Place the puppy on a rough bath towel on your lap. This surface allows the puppy to dig in with its hindquarters and gain traction, enabling it to "knead" with its front legs while it is nursing. We find using this method most closely approximates natural nursing and has been the most successful, causing the fewest problems in the long run.

The puppy may not accept the nipple at first and you may have to gently open its mouth. Make sure the puppy's tongue is at the bottom of the mouth so that it can suck properly. It will be easier to insert the nipple into the puppy's mouth if the nipple is squeezed flat.

These Corgi pups will bring happiness to new homes, because the breeder has found responsible owners for them before their dam was bred.

If the puppy does not start sucking immediately, squeeze a few drops of milk into its mouth. Usually a taste of what is yet to come will inspire most puppies to start sucking in earnest. Still, there is the reluctant pup that is bound and determined that Mom is the only way to go, and you will have to be a bit more persistent and patient. Be sure to keep the bottle tilted at an angle so that the nipple is continually filled with milk, as you do not want the puppy to suck in air.

Newborn puppies need small quantities of food, often. The average newborn Corgi puppy will consume about a half ounce of formula at

As the dam spends more and more time away from her puppies, they grow to depend on you. This six-week-old pup has been weaned to a puppy diet.

each feeding. Healthy puppies' appetites will increase in small increments every day or so. They will usually pull back and turn their heads when satisfied. As long as their abdomens seem firm and filled, but not bloated, they are doing just fine. If a puppy seems gaunt and is not gaining weight, consult your veterinarian.

Syringe-feeding

Many breeders use the syringe method of hand-feeding newborn puppies because it is so easy to control the rate of formula flow even for those middle-of-the-night feedings when you may not be fully awake. Use an insulin syringe with the needle discarded.

Place the puppy on a bath towel and gently open the puppy's mouth with one hand using the thumb and index finger. Place a drop at a time on the center and back of the puppy's tongue. When the puppy begins to swallow, add another drop or two. Most puppies will take to the procedure very quickly and begin to swallow with little difficulty. You can then very slowly increase the flow.

Tube-feeding

Tube-feeding is a great time-saving method that is especially useful when there are a good number of puppies that must be fed. A tube is inserted into the puppy's stomach through the mouth and formula is inserted into the tube with a syringe.

This is not a technique for anyone to attempt without instruction. Your veterinarian can teach you how to feed this way and will be able to supply all the equipment you will need to do so properly.

This method insures you each puppy receives the proper amount of formula and is especially helpful for the puppy that is a reluctant nurser. Do not attempt to tube-feed until you are confident you can do it correctly.

Special Care of Hand-fed Puppies

If you are completely taking over for the puppies' mother you will have to perform the functions the mother normally assumes. Clean the puppies' mouth of any milk that has accumulated there with a piece of cotton slightly dampened with warm water. Using another swab, gently rub around the area from which the puppies urinate to stimulate them to pass water. This also must be done under

A length of tube that reaches from the puppy's mouth down into the stomach is properly marked so that it is not inserted too far.

the abdomen and around the anal region, encouraging the puppies to empty their bowels.

When this has been accomplished, rub these same areas with a very small amount of Vaseline to avoid chafing and irritation. This procedure must be repeated every time the puppies are bottle-fed.

Obviously, this procedure is going to take a significant amount of time. Hand-rearing puppies is no mean feat, especially during the first two weeks when the newborn whelps must be fed every two hours. After the second week,

The tube is very carefully inserted into the puppy's stomach.

feeding times may be spaced to two-and-a-half to three hours apart. By the end of the third week, you can begin introducing the orphans to solid food.

Using Caution

Puppies that have been nursing on their mother's milk will have derived a degree of natural immunity from her that will last several weeks and after which they will need individual immunization. Puppies that have been completely hand-raised will not have this immunity and must be protected from coming in contact with any of the airborne contagious diseases.

Weaning

At about ten or twelve days old, most puppies' eyes will have begun to open. Weaning of hand-fed puppies can begin at this time but if the litter has been nursing on their mother, it is suggested by some animal behaviorists that weaning not begin until the puppies are 28 days old. Their reason for this is that puppies are extremely sensitive to abrupt changes of any kind between the ages of 21 to 28 days. Weaning can be extremely stressful to puppies before this age, so it is best to avoid doing so if not absolutely necessary.

At ten days to two weeks, even the most diligent mother is spending progressively more time away from her puppies—her little angels are rapidly developing needlelike teeth and can be quite tyrannical in having their needs met.

As this happens, it is time for you to step in and offer a hand. The easiest way to assist the transition of puppies from entire dependency upon their mother to a self-sufficient state is to allow the transition to happen gradually.

Puppy Chows

There are now good-quality puppy chows available that can be soaked and made into an easily digestible mixture from the first day of weaning. You can use cow's milk, goat's milk, or any one of a number of commercial brands prepared especially for dogs.

Mother should have some outdoor time while you are feeding her puppies or she will eat what you have put down and then regurgitate the food for the puppies. This is a natural instinct of canine mothers as their offspring come toward the end of their nursing phase and are ready to eat on their own.

It is not unusual to see a nursing mother regurgitate her own food for her puppies, especially if she is fed and then allowed to immediately return to the puppies. Most humans find this a disturbing and offensive habit, but it is not harmful to the puppies in any way unless the mother has passed back large lumps of meat or other solid food. To avoid this, it is best to keep the mother away from her puppies for at least an hour after she has eaten.

Friends of ours invented an ingenious way of feeding their new litter. The individual food dishes were placed inside a cardboard box from which the top had been removed. Round holes were cut for each puppy along the sides of the box, very close to the bottom. The puppies put their heads through the holes up to their shoulders. This not only keeps each puppy at its own dish but also saves hours of clean-up by keeping the puppies from taking a bath in their food.

Raising the Litter

Once the puppies are completely weaned, they should learn to eat from separate dishes. It is not unusual to have one or two bullies in the litter who stand in the communal food pan and intimidate a more reticent littermate. Separate dishes will allow you to see how much each puppy is eating and to feed the slow eater alone if necessary. The puppies should be fed four times a day starting first thing in the morning and about every four to five hours thereafter. At least three of these meals should be semisolid food and the other one or two meals can consist of milk with perhaps a small amount of baby cereal or premium puppy kibble added.

Corgi puppies need to be treated for roundworms beginning at three or four weeks of age. Your veterinarian will prescribe the proper treatment and the frequency of subsequent wormings.

We have always maintained the best place for the puppy playpen is in the kitchen, where there is constant traffic and all kinds of odd noises. If there are children in the household, teach them how to play with the puppies gently. All these things will add up to a well-socialized puppy, ready to go off to its new owners and provide them with years of friendship and entertainment.

You will have done your job well.

INFORMATION

Kennel Clubs and Organizations

American Herding Breed
  Association
Linda C. Rorem
1548 Victoria Way
Pacifica, CA 94044
(415) 355-9563

American Kennel Club
260 Madison Avenue
New York, NY 10016
(212) 696-8200

All Registration Information:
American Kennel Club
5580 Centerview Drive
Raleigh, NC 27606
(919) 233-9767

Cardigan Welsh Corgi Club of
  America, Inc.
Ms. Genny Conway
Corresponding Secretary
14511 Trophy Club Road
Houston, Texas 77095-3420

Cardigan Welsh Corgi Rescue
  League
H. Pamela Allen
406 East Alexandria Avenue
Alexandria, VA 22301
(703) 836-1963

Australian National Kennel
  Council
Royal Showgrounds
Ascot Vale 3032
Victoria, Australia

Canadian Kennel Club
89 Skyway Avenue, Unit 100
Etobicoke, Ontario
Canada M9W 6R4
(416) 675-5511

The Kennel Club (England)
1-5 Clargis Street
Piccadilly, London W1Y 8AB
England

New Zealand Kennel Club
Private Bag 59003
Porirua, Wellington, New Zealand

Pembroke Welsh Corgi Club of
  America
Joan Gibson Reid
Corresponding Secretary
9589 Sheldon Road
Elk Grove, CA 95624
(916) 689-1661
E-mail: jgrcorgi@aol.com

Pembroke Corgi Club of America
  Rescue League
Debbie Oliver
11429 Clayton Road
San Jose, CA 95127-5009
(408) 258-4463
Fax: (408) 258-8709

United Kennel Club
100 E. Kilgore Road
Kalamazoo, MI 49001-5598
(616) 343-9020

Books

Albin, Dickie. *The Family Welsh Corgi*. London, England: Popular Dogs Publishing Co., 1970.
Cardigan Welsh Corgi Club of America, Inc. *The Illustrated Standard of the Cardigan Welsh Corgi*. Houston, TX: Cardigan Welsh Corgi Club of America.
Fiennes, Alice and Richard. *The Natural History of Dogs*. Garden City, NY: The Natural History Press, 1970.
Harper, Deborah S. *The New Complete Pembroke Welsh Corgi*. New York, NY: Howell Book House, 1994.
Johnston, John. *Corgis in Australia*. Queensland, Australia: Pumpkin Books, 1985.
Lister-Kaye, Charles and Dickie Albin. *The Welsh Corgi*. Lon-

don, England: Popular Dogs Publishing Co. Ltd., 1979.
Pembroke Welsh Corgi Club of America, *An Illustrated Study of the Pembroke Welsh Corgi Standard*. San Jose, CA: Pembroke Welsh Corgi Club of America, 1975.

Periodicals

AKC Gazette
260 Madison Avenue
New York, NY 10016
(212) 696-8390
www.akc.org/gaztoc.htm

Bloodlines
United Kennel Club
100 E. Kilgore Road
Kalamazoo, MI 49001-5598
(616) 343-9020
www.ukcdogs.com

Dog World
29 North Wacker Drive
Chicago, IL 60606
(312) 726-2802
www.dogworldmag.com

Dogs in Canada
Apex Publishers
89 Skyway Ave. #200
Etobicoke, Ontario
Canada M9W-6R4
(416) 798-9778
www.dogs-in-canada.com

National Stockdog Magazine
P.O. Box 402
3597 CR 75
Butler, IN
(219) 868-2670

Purebred Dogs in Review
P.O. Box 30430
Santa Barbara, CA 93313
(805) 692-2055
www.dogrevu.com

INDEX

Cover Photos

Tara Darling: front, inside front, inside back, and back covers.

Photo Credits

Elizabeth Flynn: pages 4, 102; Joan Ludwig: page 7; Gunnar Lindgren: pages 8, 9; Arni: page 12; Bonnie Nance, pages 18, 31, 39 top, 64; Perry Phillips: page 16; Isabelle Francais: pages 7 bottom, 23 top, 26, 39 bottom, 42 top, 46, 60, 67, 71, 86, 94, 110, 117 bottom; Judith E. Strom: page 42 bottom, 49, 99 top right, bottom left and right; Myrna Bazzell: page 43 bottom; Tara Darling: pages 17 top, 23 bottom, 78, 90, 117 top, 120; Norvia Behling: pages 34, 52, 74, 83, 91, 99 top left, 107; Gail Bates: page 38; Kent and Donna Dannen, pages 53, 56, 66, 71, 98, 106, 121; Kitten Rodwell: page 82; Greenwood and Rodgers: pages 2, 30, 70, 125; Elaine Brower: page 113; Sharon Eide: page 116 left, right; all other photos by author; postcard on page 6 provided by author.

About the Author

Richard G. Beauchamp has been involved with purebred dogs as a breeder and exhibitor for more than 40 years. He has judged all breeds in every major country of the world and written about dogs and dog breeding for publications in many countries including Australia, England, and America. He has imported, owned, bred, and shown championship-caliber Pembroke Welsh Corgis since 1983.

Acknowledgments

The author wishes to thank the many Corgi fanciers throughout the world who so generously contributed their experiences, advice, and photographs to this project.

Important Note

This pet owner's guide tells the reader how to buy and care for a Welsh Corgi. The author and the publisher consider it important to point out that the advice given in the book is meant primarily for normally developed puppies from a good breeder—that is, dogs of excellent physical health and good temperament.

Anyone who adopts a fully grown dog should be aware that the animal has already formed its basic impressions of human beings. The new owner should watch the animal carefully, including its behavior toward humans, and should meet the previous owner. If the dog comes from a shelter, it may be possible to get some information on the dog's background and peculiarities there. There are dogs that, for whatever reason, behave in an unnatural manner or may even bite. Under no circumstances should a known "biter" or an otherwise ill-tempered dog be adopted or purchased as a pet or show prospect.

Caution is further advised in the association of children with dogs, in meeting with other dogs, and in exercising the dog without a leash.

Even well-behaved and carefully supervised dogs sometimes do damage to someone else's property or cause accidents. It is therefore in the owner's interest to be adequately insured against such eventualities, and we strongly urge all dog owners to purchase a liability policy that covers their dog.

All inquiries should be addressed to:
Barron's Educational Series, Inc.
250 Wireless Boulevard
Hauppauge, NY 11788

http://www.barronseduc.com

Library of Congress Catalog Card No. 98-31185

ISBN-13: 978-0-7641-0557-9
ISBN-10: 0-7641-0557-4

Library of Congress Cataloging-in-Publication Data
Beauchamp, Richard G.
    Welsh corgis : Pembroke and Cardigan / Richard
G. Beauchamp ; illustrations by Pam Tanzey.
        p.   cm. — (A Complete pet owner's manual)
        Includes bibliographical references (p. 124)
and index.
        ISBN 0-7641-0557-4
        1. Pembroke Welsh corgi. 2. Cardigan Welsh
corgi. I. Title. II. Series.
SF429.P33B435   1999
636.737—dc21   98-31185
                                          CIP

Printed in China
18 17 16 15 14 13 12 11

The two Welsh Corgis—Pembroke and Cardigan—are separate and distinct breeds, each with a fascinating history and a loyal following. Both are herding dogs, and love to perform the job for which their breeds were developed, whether it's on a working farm or in herding trials, a sport enjoyed by increasing numbers of Corgis and their owners. If a Corgi is in your future, plan ahead for plenty of activity. Agility and Flyball are two fast-paced sports you can enjoy with your Pembroke or Cardigan—both intelligent, good natured, companions that require early, consistent training to realize their potential.